# CROWN

## HER STORY • HER POWER • HER VOICE

Compiled by Natima Sheree

Cover Illustration by L. Butler

Published by: Transparent Gem Inc.

ISBN: 979-8417744907

Printed in the United States of America

First Edition

This anthology is dedicated to all the brave women who are battling societal pressures and fighting to be seen and heard. Raise your heads Queen, no longer will you be silenced or ignored... this is your *Crown Assist!*

# Contents

# Foreword

Stop the Queenocide! I said what I said. Stop. The. Queenocide. Queens are enlisting in the army of the living dead at an alarming rate. No basic training needed – we already know how to take a sister out. Our bloodhound instincts kick in, and we begin to sniff. We sniff out Queens with low self-esteem because we can. We sniff out Queens making power moves because we feel threatened. We roam the streets with our assault rifles locked and loaded, licking our chops and taking shots: you think you're cute – you ain't shit – who the hell do you think you are? With every shot fired, we destroy our target. Sometimes the target is our self: I'm not good enough – nobody wants me – I don't matter.

We're wearing the wrong helmet, y'all. This homicidal, genocidal, suicidal, QUEENOCIDAL mentality has got to cease! Yeah, we may look good, but until we address the mess beneath the crown, we will continue this debilitating warfare against each other until our realm of influence lies in ruins and we are taken away captive once and for all.

It starts with a mirror facing moment – a moment where we look past the beat face, the weave, the piercings, the tattoos, the thug-ruggedness, the diva-tude and acknowledge that there is anger and fear and self-loathing, bitterness and trauma and trauma response. We have to take a deep breath, embrace our brokenness and admit that we need to heal - that to facilitate our healing, we need help. Now, I know what you're thinking so PUMP.YOUR.BRAKES.

Seeking help is not a sign of weakness. Sis, you are not weak; your crown is heavy! It is not a physical crown of which I speak. Your deity, your royalty is within – for your crown is your purpose, and it is 24 carat platinum, not 24-ounce tin! The glory that becomes visible radiates from within. That's heavy, and we all know that heavy needs help to lift. Imagine what would happen if we all put down our assault rifles and put our hands to better use – like say a crown assist?

This anthology is our crown assist to you. It is our hope that our stories will help you to help yourself, and in turn, to help someone else. We share our experiences to assist you in reconciling the things beneath your crown. We share so that in your mirror facing moments, you know you aren't alone.

Let's commit to doing the work necessary to normalize self-affirmation and positivity. Let's finish our tours of duty and never re-enlist. Let us take off the helmet, wear our crowns proudly, and put the Queenocide to rest.

*Nancy Marie*

# Her Story

# Tethered Faith

## Samentha Moore

*"This feeling will one day be a distant memory
and a humble reminder..."*

## Act Two

Then, one day, you wake up and it's the first day of the rest of your life. Nothing like what you had ever envisioned. Here I was, a single mom with my newly gained freedom, starting from absolutely nothing. Like, for real, nothing. Hopeful to heal and rebuild, the starting point felt unclear. Having put all my focus on surviving and escaping a toxic marriage, the next steps felt tandemly far away and imminent.

Balancing my new life and the feelings that came to the surface was exhausting. I walked around feeling bitter and angry over the past. I was in a dark place, resentment and depression set in and I felt like I was under ten tons of brick, trying to break through. Anytime I saw a crack of light, another ton would fall. Nothing was feeling right; I was in a place of life discomfort.

Then, it was clear that the prayers that I was crying out for daily were being answered. Praying for renewed faith, wisdom, healing, a changed mindset, freedom, peace and happiness.

It was growing pains. I hated them. But the thing with wisdom is, once you gain insight, it will not go away. I tried to ignore it. Then the season comes where you have to make the intentional decision to truly heal, dig deep and do the work. I was tired of being
exhausted for what felt like no reason. Trying to control everything *is* exhausting!

I decided to do "the work."

The work is relative. It is a tailored path for each one of us, but what is true for us all is that we have to commit to the process.

When you live in a mindset of lack for so long, it warps how you see yourself and what you think you are capable of. With my newfound life, a reassessment of every part of it was necessary. I turned from survival mode to purpose driven and that was the hardest part!

God reveals all the things. Like, *all* the things! My prayer was that God renew me from the inside out and grant me the grace to walk in it. To mold my desires to reflect His will for my life.

That is exactly what He did. Now, it was up to me to be obedient and do it. That self-accountability hits hard. You have to do a lot of what you don't want to do. When you are convicted to look at yourself and make the necessary changes to live a life of worth, it
is humbling.

I was so used to living in an erratic environment for so long, that when everything fell apart, I became controlling over the things in my life that I thought I could control. I never wanted to

feel the uneasiness of being out of control and unsafe again. My trust issues ran so deeply that they affected my trust and faith. I had allowed my disappointing experiences with humans to taint my relationship
with God.

God was telling me that He wanted me to give Him myself and my life fully, that He didn't need my help. What He needed was for me to let go and get out of the way.

Throughout this chapter, I want to share a bit of what my personal and continuous journey of rebuilding has looked like, the highs and lows of it. You will also see entries from my journals and devotionals throughout the years. My hope is to share and encourage you to keep on going through your journey.

*"The season that I'm in right now is the hardest I've been through. The loneliness, fatigue, shortcomings, lack of security—in what feels like in every way. These verses (Psalms 71:20-21) really struck me, made me remember that life is a series of ups and downs, but what remains the same is God's love and comfort. And what a privilege to know that with each trial, He increases my honor. There is an increase within my pain."*

## Pray, Then Pray Some More

My prayer life got stale. I was in a place where I thought God was mad at me, and if we are being honest, I was mad at God! I felt disconnected. I started just praying what felt like a script. Being a church kid, it was out of habit.

I was wrestling with my own guilt from getting a divorce. Even though my marriage far from honored God, I still felt like I had failed. Now I was a single mother, and I felt like that was even more judgement that I would have to face. Because I felt that way, I didn't feel that I was worthy of a relationship with God or that any word that I uttered went past my ceiling.

*"Revelation 8:3-4: The devil does not want me to know how precious my prayers are to God. When I pray, it takes things out of my hands and puts them in His. This is my time to admit that I am no longer leaning onto my own understanding. I will not receive it, if I do not ask. I have to ask. Praying is not just for when life is hard, it is for all times."*

## Finding My Intuition (Again)

Reconnecting with my intuition was of major importance to me. I spent years ignoring it and being told what I was feeling was invalid. My gut, that had been with me my entire life, felt like a stranger. I would question my intuition with simple things, like when it came to giving someone a call or a text if they crossed my mind. Or bigger things, like not moving forward with certain relationships or even professional opportunities.

I had to learn to trust myself enough to listen to how I was feeling. Something that seemed so small made a huge impact on my life. Getting to a place where I was settled and trusting of my judgement was a complete blessing.

## Me, Myself and I...Then Everyone Else

You have to know yourself in order to know how to relate to others. If we don't, we live a life that is one-dimensional and shallow.

We all would like to think that we know ourselves, and for the most part, we know "of" ourselves. For me, over time, I became like a broken mirror that was merely a reflection of others in my life. I molded myself into a palpable version of myself that I felt may be easier for others to digest. I created a "clean" version of myself rooted in the fear of rejection and not being fully accepted. Living a life that was geared towards making others happy, not even considering myself.

Things had to change. I had to give myself the love that I felt was lacking in my life. How could I allow someone else to someday love me, if that was something that I could not even give to myself? How could I know what to focus on if I didn't know where I was going? I needed to be clear about my purpose and where I was going before anything else.

*"Lord, help me to truly see and accept myself. I pray that with each passing day, I am able to understand that I am worth all the greatness in life. I want to truly wake up every morning grateful for the gift of another day. To not expect, function or accept that feeling of dread that I sadistically fell into. That failure and disappointment is not in my actions or expectations of others. I want God's confidence to permeate through every cell of my body. I want to breathe, be present and reject negative thoughts. I want to continue to learn and understand just how much God is in every decision and action I make. I just want to grow in knowledge and understanding. I confidently ask and expect the Lord for His wisdom. I walk into the remainder of this week positive, excited and grateful. I pray for bountiful blessings. You are with me."*

## Therapy Is for the Strong

There I was, able to redefine what healing looked like for me. To heal at my own pace and with just myself in mind and heart.

Deciding to start my life over was just one step. I held onto resentment because I was so exhausted, and life was still requiring me to do so much. I just wanted to rest. Feeling like I had to show up in my life in a million ways, I felt like I was

cracking
under pressure.

My therapist told me, "You're a perfectionist, and you have to go easy on yourself." I was not willing to hear that. I was not a perfectionist, because to me, so much had already gone so wrong. How could I be a perfectionist?

After sitting with it and looking at my life patterns, I came to my own realization that I truly was. I had spent the better part of my life up until then living a quiet life of hurt behind closed doors yet retaining an image of happiness on the outside. I was a self-proclaimed self-soother, oftentimes taking my losses in silence.

I didn't have to do that anymore; I took my freedom to live in truth and share my testimony. And we can see a lot of our reflection when we give ourselves the freedom to speak and live our truths.

*"Psalm 126:6: This verse tells me that there is always work to be done. It doesn't say those who go out weeping return with songs of joy, it says those who go out weeping, carrying seeds to sow, will return with songs of joy. This to me is saying to push through, to hang on and keep grinding. That He sees me. This also shows me that it's ok to show vulnerability, so long as it is edifying. The scripture says to go out weeping, to me that means face the world during suffering and struggle. Being transparent during my valley season and sharing my testimony with others. This verse really blesses me and speaks to where I am right now in my life."*

## (Self) Forgiveness

I got to a place where I was so beaten down in what seemed like every area of my life. I was so hurt and disappointed from life that my trust issues became bigger than my faith. I was hurt from

transferring the love and attention I needed from God onto others. I was controlling all that I could in my life, leaving little room
for faith.

When I was eight years old and had accepted the Lord into my life, I'd had childlike faith. I was hopeful, confident and trusting. I knew I needed to get back to that. Back to that faith that was so strong, no one could shake me or tell me otherwise.

I took the time to not only acknowledge what I was feeling, but to peel layers back and get to the root of who I was, am and will become. Find the core of why I was feeling the way I was and decide what I wanted and deserved. Repairing and re-parenting myself.

I started taking baby steps towards healing my inner child wounds and sitting in self-reflection. Scouring ways that I myself had been toxic and stunted. Making more mindful decisions to take responsibility and correct those ways. Creating space to forgive myself and promising to do better.

That was the difficult part. Being so hard on myself the way that I was, I was giving out that same energy to everyone else. Reassessing any and all relationships, I decided that I was going to let go of expectations and allow people to be who they were. If that didn't align with where God was taking me, that was ok. I decided to be grateful for the connection, no matter how short or long it was and learn as much from it as I could.

I secluded myself for a while and got to reacclimate myself to myself again and in many ways, introduced myself to myself. I started making lists, lists of things I wanted to do and experience, and places I wanted go; things I desired in my lifetime.

Always having lived in a codependent space, I stepped out in anxious faith and started doing these things by myself.

## From Agitation to Obedience

Speak your truth with trusted sources and put a plan into action. I was at my wits end with my job; I was so sick and tired of feeling like I was in a hamster wheel. I was at the point where it just wasn't enough. It wasn't just monetary, it was the energy, the purpose, and the characters. It all felt missing.

Noticing parallels from my past personal life and my current career life, I'd had enough. I was overworked, underpaid and under-appreciated, and the worst was being underutilized. Knowing what I had to offer was one thing but knowing that there were others that were well informed and exposed to my capabilities and were actively trying to squander that was the ultimate disrespect. Expecting a lot for very little in return.

It wasn't just for me to notice anymore, I had to position myself to be ready for greater things. I remember crying every day on the way to work and every day driving home. I had nothing to lose at that point. Living in the grips of depression, anxiety, and stress, I was ready for an intentional shift.

I had to consciously turn my agitation to obedience, and that was difficult and extremely lonely at times. I knew that if I lived in obedience, intense obedience, that God would reward me. The pain came from not knowing how or when, but that is also where the faith came in. Not knowing when but knowing it would happen. I knew that my deliverance was going to come directly from my obedience, so that meant that I had to filter out all distractions and just focus on the things that I knew God was calling me to do.

God gave me an out, but it came with a cost. For a season, I made the choice to sacrifice all of my days off from one job in order to make room for where I prayed for Him to take me. I used every day off and every vacation day pouring into an opportunity that I knew was God-given. I was tired, exhausted, but for the first time in a while, I was feeling fulfilled.

*"I pray for things, and cling to God to show my faith, but I definitely leave Him out to dry after the novelty of the blessing runs out. Back to wanting and asking more and clinging to Him. I want my fervency to be consistent and keep striving for that. The men knew that Jesus was coming and met him. He healed them and nine of the men bounced. I can't even judge because I know that's what I often do to him. But the blessing isn't even really in the healing, it's in the praise afterwards. And praise is an act of faith."*

## One Tenth

I always tithed, but I was never consistent. Growing up in the church, I was always aware about tithing, but I can't say that I had a personal attachment to it. It was always more of an "option" for me than a habit. If money was tight—and trust me, it was for a while—tithing was the first thing to go. Even when I did, it wasn't always first fruits or a full ten percent.

I was sitting in church one day, and a guest pastor preached on tithing. I was convicted in a new way, shifting my mentality to give even when I don't have, or when I *think* I don't have enough. To continue to bless, sow and pour into others in the seasons where and when I find that I need it too. That the more I trusted God with what I had and ultimately what He blessed me with, the more He had room to bless me.

I stopped controlling and started trusting, giving my first to Him, before anything else, no matter what I was facing financially. I learned that for me, the act of tithing was giving God the space to do what He said He would. It was more or less a challenge, and He never fails. As I tithed, I prayed—and still continue to pray—that He would continue to bless me financially and guide me on how to be a good steward of what I am given. Trusting that He could do more with 90% than I could ever do with 100% myself.

*"Sow when I don't have it. This is a commitment and a lifestyle. When I sow, I must be patient and wait for the harvest. I will reap something! I can keep my abundance of joy, even in my deepest of pressure and poverty because my joy is not indicative of the circumstances around me. When I learn to give beyond my ability, God will take me beyond my ability. He will bless me in ways unimaginable. I need to give with urgency and understand that my breakthrough and miracle are tied to my sowing."*

## Relationships

Every relationship is important. We focus too much on romantic relationships, not giving enough credit to how day-to-day relationships and friendships alter our perception and lives. These are the people that we trust, confide and pray with/for.

Any energetic exchange is affecting you, whether we want to acknowledge it or not. Sometimes, we use others as distractions to the work that we need to be doing ourselves. We transfer what we need to be doing for ourselves onto others.

Relationships aren't about what others can do for you, or where others can take you. But more about the peace and edification they bring to your life, and vice versa. Evaluating and re-evaluating exactly why you are in any relationship and if it is continually edifying. As Brene Brown said in her book, *Daring Greatly*, "Take a 1-inch x 1-inch square of paper and make a list of people whose opinions matter to you—those people who love you, not in spite of, but because of your vulnerabilities and imperfections." Brown says, "If you need more paper, you need to edit."[1]

This started helping me shift my mindset and who I was giving my power to. If they truly had no immediate impact on mine or my child's life, then I needed to honor that. I needed to refocus my energy into caring about what my opinion of myself was first and foremost.

*"This has nothing to do with anyone but me. I've put other relationships above my relationship with God for years. That's why I'm feeling the pain I do now. Consequences to my decisions. I understand that. I understand that now. I've never taken the time to admit it. I don't want to feel this way. I don't want to think this way. I want to be healthy. I want to have healthy relationships and attachments.*

*"I want to die to myself and truly live for the Lord. No more false idols. No more seeking the kind of love that I can only get from God, from humans. I'll never find that there. I am being held so close to God. I can feel it. I feel saved. Wrapped in His arms.*

*"I repent for my broken ways and understanding of the world. I repent for asking God to bless my plans and not honestly seeking His. I want to open my entire heart and life to God and do his work. I don't want to be so scared of opening up and fellowshipping with others that I cling so desperately and insecurely to the few that I do have. That is abusive.*

[1] Brene Brown. *Daring Greatly.* Penguin Putnam Inc. (New York, United States); September 11th, 2012.

*"No more Godly expectations in a human world. It hurts God, me and all involved. That is not the light I choose to emit. The energy I am willing to share. I am loved. Madly loved. My sin... all my sin has been covered and erased because I am that worth it.*

*"No more living day to day looking to be validated by the actions or words of another other than my God. I will seek Him. I pray for the strength to continue to connect in this space, to learn my lesson*
*and grow.*

*"I rebuke anger, judgment, hatred, resentment, hurt, blame, self-hate, expectations, jealousy, envy, abusive mentality, fear, anxiety, depression, doubt, brokenness, insecurities and low sel-0worth. I am loved to the max already. I've been. By the only one that matters. And I'm not mad."*

## Valuable Self-Correction

After much self-healing and assessment, I realized that it was me that was the common denominator in all my situations. Not only was it me, but it was all attached to what I felt like I deserved. I was so wrapped up in my worth being predicated on what others thought about me and how they treated me, that I began to think on the same toxic wavelength. I realized that I was the constant and I needed to change what that looked like. I no longer would allow lukewarm relationships or habitual tasks to take up space in my life, distracting me from what God truly had for me.

I wasn't scared anymore. I wasn't scared to be alone; I actually started to like it. I was able to live my life, tend to my energy, give myself experiences and release any feelings of anxious attachment and codependency that I had been used to.

Changing my constant was the best thing I did, because I was giving myself the space to honor myself and my truth. I no longer feared creating boundaries that would push people away. It is ok to know the depth of how far you want to engage with someone and guard your heart. Being open to things developing into a deeper connection is fine, but healthy boundaries is key to peace of mind. Keeping professional relationships professional and personal relationships personal helped me.

I learned as I matured that I have a magnetic personality, but that does not mean that everyone or anyone can have access to me. That was the point when I realized that those who truly cared and edified me would honor my boundaries, and I'd do the same towards them.

*"I slept better last night. But it was a struggle to make sure my mind didn't wander off into stressful territory as I slipped off to sleep. I woke up feeling hopeful and grasping for positivity. I did morning meditation and listened to my positive affirmations. I am going to have a great day. I need to change and commit to how I start my days. I need to worry about myself and my wellbeing. Nothing else. There is a thin line between "fake it until you make it" and straight up fake. I'm trying to find my balance between acknowledging my feelings but not staying there, and it'll take time. I think my therapist will really help me with that."*

## Scary Success

As terrified as I was of failure, I was petrified of success. Even as God gave me glimpses of my future—clear glimpses— they felt so out of reach, I dismissed them. Afraid of what life would be like if they actually happened.

So used to toxicity and dysfunction, I became afraid of what my responsibility would be in order to attain and retain His blessings. I had faith, but it was limited to my "realistic" beliefs, all rooted in my hurt and pain.

God was giving me pieces of the big picture on purpose. He was challenging me to faith my way to it. He said, "It's yours, but you have to truly believe."

I was living in a perpetual state of fearing that "the other shoe would drop." That I was living on autopilot. Not believing in God's power enough to use me and my life as a miracle. My heart was so delicate, I would have rather lived a basic life than risked living beyond my dreams and imagination. I was so fearful of another disappointment because I was positive that I wouldn't recover.

What I learned in this season was how to live in active faith. To get specific. To pray about *everything*. It was no longer enough to think about the glimpses. I had to get specific and pray about the details that God blessed me with. No detail was too small.

## Meditate

I started to meditate. This took me a long time to implement in my life. Being still in silence did not work well for an A-type planner like me. My mind goes a mile a second and it felt like it was not an efficient use of the little time I already felt that I had.

I was so wrong! Meditation actually made me feel like I had more time. There is so much healing in stillness.

Meditation can look different for everyone. For me, sometimes I sit in my meditation room in complete silence. Other times, I use a guided meditation on an app, or meditation music. And sometimes I put on praise and worship music and just cry.

Meditation is a beautiful space to not live in any moment but the present. We are always trying to lament over the past or strategize the future, but the present is where we can make the

most impact. Giving myself the gift of active rest made a big difference in my mindset
and perspective.

## Just Breathe

I was well into my healing and wellness journey, hungry for more opportunities to release and rebuild. I found a community, just for black women, led by black women, to be vulnerable and to do healing breathwork. (Breathwork is conscious breathing that promotes healing, releases trauma and grounds the spirit.)

I made the investment, for and by myself, to go to an in-person group session and it was absolutely amazing. We took time to journal a few prompts and we did a group breathing session.

The most powerful part for me was the end when we were given the space to scream. And when I say scream, I mean the loudest screams I could muster up. Years of locked in anxiety, stress, anger and energy was released. It was freeing and amazing, I felt lighter and renewed. This was a practice I knew I was going to implement in my self-care regimen.

*"I have so much going on in my mind; it never stops. This past week, I have made it my duty to be positive and present. I'm exhausted. I'm changing every day. I'm trying to stop being anal and go with the flow, while being present and in control. I hate this feeling of loneliness and anxiety. It's debilitating, but I have been having much better*
*days because I am choosing to. I am choosing to see God in every little thing."*

## Intentional Affirmations

I needed to start intentionally loving myself. So, I started doing affirmations. I did affirmations like it was medicinal. Let me tell you, it felt *weird* at first! Looking at myself in the mirror and saying, "I love all of me," or, "I am not lazy about my healing."

Before I had never given myself that type of attention, but then it shifted over time. I found that throughout my day, I would repeat this to myself, as well as several other affirmations. I wrote them down and taped them in several places in my house: my coffee table, bathroom, bedroom and office. I had an app on my phone that ensured I always had an active affirmation up.

This small habit made a huge change in my life. I started to truly consider and uplift myself. I started feeling the intuition that I thought I had lost after years of gaslighting. I found her, and I truly loved her and became protective of myself at any cost.

## Delayed Blessings

The waiting season can be incredibly difficult. I felt forgotten, abandoned and angry. Relationships shifted and truths came to light. The waiting season is a season of major growth, and what I was feeling was stretching me in unimaginable ways.

Embracing the delay and living in active faith allowed me to live in desperate delay. I wrote in my journal even when it hurt so badly, I could physically feel the pain. Seeing those feelings on paper just does something. For me, it is a marker of humbleness, staying grounded and accountability.

Even now, when I read my entries from years ago—snippets that you are reading in this very chapter—I can taste the heartbreak, hurt and pain I was healing through. It makes me so grateful for where God has brought me since and excited about where He still plans to take me. Living a life that I was once merely manifesting, I was living clear evidence of God's grace and mercy.

## Continued Journey

What pride and ego makes us do is wait until we are past a valley or have moved a mountain before sharing with others, if we even share at all. We feel that we need to have the beginning, middle and ending before we can truly impact others. That is far from the truth, and a lie that Satan would have us believe.

Us sharing our troubles, struggles and doubts is what shows others God's grace and mercy. There is never an "end point" with healing journeys; we will always be maturing our way through life.

Not one person is perfect, and we should not expect to be, but we can always strive for it. That is exactly what sanctification is; the action or process of being freed or purified. We know we will not ever get to perfection, but we become refined individuals as
we strive.

Stop playing small; the things that are worth it oftentimes come with a series of challenges. That does not mean for you to give up! Life has ups and downs, mountains and valleys. I can't tell you what the future holds, but I can assure you that I am going to polish my crown and let my faith lead the way.

# Unconditionally Her:
# A Queen from Queens

## Natima Sheree

It was important to me to not only compile but to contribute to this body of work, and so as I began to prepare my chapter, I was thoughtful about what I wanted to write. What stories I would tell, what experiences I would share and what words I would use to edify and motivate you. I wanted to be sure my story and contribution was transparent, relatable, and real. I wanted people to read my words and understand why my passion for women empowerment and sisterhood is so strong. Why everything I've done in my adult life has been to help others; and writing this chapter is no different.

As much as I would love to entertain you or make you laugh, I'd much rather prompt resolute thoughts that lead to introspection and eventually toward action and changed behavior. Now this is not a judgement or assumption that there is something wrong with your current habits, but if you've picked up this book, it is likely you were looking for personal development advice, or inspiration.

There are millions of books available that teach self-help, and introspection; but the writer often starts the story of empowerment from their own place of wholeness, long after the hurt, and pain, that prompted their growth journey in the first place, has subsided. Now don't get me wrong, there is no fault or flaw in this method of storytelling or teaching; in fact, its proven to be extremely effective. No one wants care from a doctor who is bleeding themselves, right? But think about how powerful and validating it would be to read a story from a perspective where a person's healing isn't totally complete, hearing an account of the raw emotion and experiences from their transformative space. That beautiful intersection in life's journey where past, present, and future all meet to reflect, reveal, and co-exist. What if you got a glimpse of someone's journey, within the journey? That road to recovery, self-discovery, and awareness.... That pivotal juncture in life I refer to as the "reclamation season." I define this as the interim between who you were, who you are, and who you are becoming. Who you are by life's design and who you were destined to be by Gods divine innovation.

That redemptive, restorative, and repurposing phase of life that presents irrefutable evidence that the diluted and/or counterfeit version of who you are now, is merely a temporary nature purposed for this transition.

Now you might be reading this thinking "I have NO clue what she's talking about!" Or you may be reading this and feeling the tears well up in your eyes because you know exactly what I'm describing and remembering when you felt it. Whichever reaction you declare, just know that this is exactly where I am... my reclamation season.

I am determined to reclaim what's mine. I'm going after the purpose and promises that were assigned to my life since the womb. I am pursuing my dreams unapologetically, fearlessly, and relentlessly. I am learning to love every flaw, and blemish, while developing the parts of me that could be better, intrinsically, or extrinsically. I'm improving the most important relationship in my life, the one with self. And then working to better how I interact and connect with others. I am committed to making the rest of my life the best of my life and taking full responsibility for my own happiness. I make gratitude a practice and priority; and I am careful to celebrate the milestones that led me to this critical interlude. I don't dwell on the hardships, or setbacks as I once did. Instead, I've learned to reflect and move forward because the very things that were supposed to crush me, are what has "crowned" me.

What I hope resonates with you most, is that beneath the crown, there is struggle, shame, and disappointment; not just the qualities that make us beautiful or significant. I want my story to teach you that failure and success are equal markers in your journey, and both serve as confirmation that there is purpose in you, and that you are on your path. I want you to be reminded that perfection is not the prerequisite to greatness, perseverance is. And that if you are willing to try, you can change anything. I hope my story serves as your "crown assist" and inspires you to invest in yourself and to discover the greatness within.

## Concrete Castle

The unique mix of urban and suburban, middle-class, and deprived; commercial, retail, and residential properties, an integrated, diverse, and emerging city where vibrant cultures intersected... this is my hometown, of Queens, New York.

The birthplace of icons and celebrities like LL Cool J, Run DMC, 50 Cent, Russell Simmons, MC Lyte, Tichina Arnold, and DJ Envy, (to name a few), and the incubate community that would nurture, influence, and lay the foundation for me to become the woman I am today.

My neighborhood was full of pride. Healthy pride. Every family on my block represented a different country, culture, and legacy with a unique set of rituals, practices, and beliefs. Living on my block was like taking a daily trip to the United Nations. Observing first and second-generation Caribbean and Latino immigrants co-exist was my norm; a unified locality that I wouldn't come to appreciate until I reached adulthood.

Aside from Asian Americans who owned the beauty supply store, nail salon and Chinese restaurants, most of the businesses in my area were owned by its residents. Before gentrification, families who owned businesses in a particular neighborhood or community usually lived there too. Our local Caribbean restaurants and international markets, barber shops, beauty salons, cab service, general store, daycare center and Montessori schools were mostly "black owned." It's interesting how according to economic and census statistics, I lived in a "disadvantaged" neighborhood just above the poverty line and yet many of the businesses in my area were owned by the black and brown people who resided there.

I learned very young that mass media delineation of an event, occurrence, or demographic isn't always accurate or true. On par with decades of intentional misrepresentation of the most beautiful, rich, and resourceful continent on the earth in textbooks, media, and film. And yes, I'm referring to Africa. Imagery that highlighted only the poor and impoverished parts of Africa, keeping cameras and illustration far from its thriving ecosystem, and its self-sustaining independence from the rest of the world. Africa isn't a poor place in need of a global savior, media just needed you to believe that, so that you'd continue to support their avarice foundations and deceptive crowd-funding campaigns. But I digress...

I was surrounded by business owners and hustlers. There was something special about the citizens of Queens, and NYC at large, a vibe that set us apart from the rest of the world. Native New Yorkers possess an innate hustle, a natural grind if you will; and irrespective of how you chose to leverage it, no one could deny they possessed it. Necessity and creativity birthed home-operated businesses as well, everything from selling dinners, to doing hair, shoveling snow, or cutting grass; whatever you needed or wanted, there was someone in my neighborhood that could supply it, provide it, or get it.

Me, I was the "candy girl!" Every day in school I had candy for sale during peak school hours. Those few hours following lunch and leading into dismissal were the most crucial. It was the interim when most students were in "energy crash mode" providing me with maximum profit opportunity. My candy supply was always in demand! I learned how to hustle from my bookbag without getting caught. I had an entire system clicking in the halls that only certain students knew about. Confirmed later in life, I knew you couldn't trust everybody with sensitive information; all it takes is one hater, one jealous peer to rat on you and blow up your whole operation. So, I was selective on who I sold to. I had a set price which included a 20% markup on what the bodegas charged. I understood supply and demand, and I knew to keep an inventory of the candy my classmates were willing to buy at a premium (sour powers, now n later, sunflower seeds, chick-o-stick, lemonheads, warheads, bazooka... and more).

At the age of 12, I thought I was just making some pocket change, but looking back I realize just how entrepreneurial my hustle was.

Although my mom and dad both had their own hustles, they were not the only ones responsible for influencing my understanding of the intricacies of strategic operations or the astute sales plan I developed as a result.

I would often watch the street pharmacists in my neighborhood, who to me, ran their stores better than some of the top CEOs we revere and respect today. I was always impressed with their ability to run and oversee multiple "lines of business" in their head from a street corner for more than 14 hours a day. Managing HR and employee relations (the corner boys), procurement (the supplier), inventory (the product), finance (the money and concealed transactions), distribution and customer service (the addicts). Now before you judge, take a minute to consider if given different choices, or opportunities who these enterprising young men might be today. I may not have agreed with their business, but I damn sure respected the infrastructure and methodologies resulting from their street smarts and instinctive business savvy.

Despite some random structural damage, litter and a few unkept yards, my neighborhood was nicer than most. I loved growing up in St. Albans; we had annual block parties, community day and "clean Queens" initiatives. We had several churches in the area, and other community-based centers for youth empowerment and development. I ran on a community track team, swam at a community pool, and attended the community summer camps. Key word was community!

I learned young the importance of connection and support. Everyone looked out for each other. I had "Aunties" and "Uncles" on my block, who weren't blood relatives but were certainly family. Neighbors that acted more like second parents, who would correct and chastise me if they witnessed any behavior outside of what I was raised to exhibit.

I was a proud Queens Girl! I had just enough sass, dope energy, and bold style to match my neighborhood; to me, I was the perfect blend of sweet and street! Most of the people knew me, my parents and family and so I felt safe for the most part. I had clashes with some of the girls in my area, but our temporary beef never kept me from a park, a party, or a carnival. I loved being outside; I could spend all day and night running the streets with my siblings and friends. We never got bored touring our community; we walked those streets a million times and yet every time we had a new experience, and a new vibe.

To this day I catch myself reminiscing about my childhood in Queens and picture the basketball and handball courts, Mr. Softee ice cream trucks, "the square," and "the rock..." those natural and artificial elements and landmarks from my neighborhood that will be etched in my mind forever, prompting feelings of nostalgia for the rest of my life.

It wasn't until young adulthood that I understood, the familiarity of my surroundings may have made me feel safe, but the limitations of travel beyond my city or neighboring cities, caused me to be narrow-minded and shortsighted. Undeniably, growing up in New York taught me to hustle, to persevere, to be a woman of my word; to appreciate culture, music, the arts, and community. It taught me how to navigate ambiguous environments with ease and how to read energy and flow in discernment. Attributes, and practices that are extremely useful and beneficial to this day; however, growing up in my neighborhood also developed in me some futile ideals, and negative behaviors.

The crime in my neighborhood was immoderate and we were taught very young to be suspicious and cautious of anyone outside of our 20-block radius. This made me extremely standoffish and closed off. I wasn't comfortable around new people and didn't like the idea of sharing my friends. I resisted change and was extremely combative and argumentative. Unaware of what my youth and naivety kept hidden from me, I can now see how my experiences developed my unconscious biases and shaped my fixed mindset. Not all my indiscreet habits or unappealing predispositions resulted from the conditions in my hood, some of it was bloodline, parental and sibling influence; but the fact that my block was filled with outspoken, and boisterous single mothers certainly did play a role.

Mine was one of five homes on the entire block that had a father present. Some of my neighbors had uncles or their mothers had boyfriends who stayed with them, but the presence of fathers was insufficient. I didn't understand why my mother would refer to a girl my age as "fast" and blame it on the absence of her father or her distracted mother. I couldn't comprehend how one thing had anything to do with the other; I guess it was because my father was around. My father's presence in my home life certainly played
a major role in my decision making, social interactions and
self-esteem.

The significance of an involved father instills a sense of security, and self-confidence. I believe my siblings and I turned out different from some of the other kids on my block because of our father's presence, protection, and counsel.

I attended public school and to me they were decent institutions. I had a few black teachers but adjusting to having mostly white teachers throughout my academic career wasn't a challenge for me. The few black teachers we did have were all female. The only black men in my elementary school were the janitors, or coaches. It wasn't until I attended I.S.59 Junior High School that I encountered a black man in leadership outside of my own home.

School was always important to me, I wouldn't admit it then, but getting good grades validated me. I would pretend not to care about school like my friends but deep down I cared a lot.

My father always told me, "*What you know is the one thing no one can ever take from you.*" He would go on to say, "*they can repossess your car, foreclose on your home, they can even unjustifiably take away your freedom, but no one can ever take-away what you know!*" My parents fought about a lot of things before and after their divorce, but one thing they could always agree upon was the importance of our education.

I can recall a time my parents got into a heated discussion with my 4th grade teacher over test results during a parent-teacher conference. My father strongly opposed using standardized tests to determine the success or trajectory of a child's future. Insensible to what was being decided for me and my future by bureaucrats who would never know anything about me beyond my aptitude for passing or failing inequitable tests, I could sense this standard was counterproductive. I do remember feeling proud though, after hearing my parents collectively defend me and my academic potential so passionately.

At that age, I was ignorant to the urban education stigmas, and stereotypes placed on children and teens growing up in my neighborhood; nor did I understand that the alarming rate of failure had less to do with the behavior, learning capabilities or grades of students, and more to do with the agenda of those funding, and regulating the school systems.

A defeatist education system was but one obstacle I would unknowingly overcome. The oversimplification of concentrated poverty, police brutality, disconnected and destructive youth, and a culture of violence has been a detriment in the inner city for decades operating as the opposer in the unconscious battle from youth to adulthood.

There is a great majority of my peers who got stuck; their arrested development was a direct result of the subliminal conditions and circumstances that surrounded us daily. The social consequences and negative developmental outcomes were intended for the young people in my city, and the underfunded and neglected public schools in my district were the catalyst.

Youth who were likely to end up in prison, addicted to drugs or alcohol, high school dropouts or unwed teen mothers would not be by accident, but by design. Diagnosing rare learning styles as problematic and creating a dependency on the pharmaceutical drugs prescribed to "control it" is by design. Serving heavily salted, processed foods in free lunch programs only to ensure students who have no choice but to ingest these meals become obese, vitamin deficient and develop poor nutrition habits. This is all by design. Canceling free arts programs or afterschool activities because of "budget cuts" leaving children and young people with no place to go but the streets. This is indeed ALL by design.

Being among those who "got out," those who made it beyond the impediments and social barricades strategically arranged to divert, and prevent our possibilities, I am immensely grateful. I don't take for granted nor do I pretend to be oblivious or impervious to the intentional destruction attempts on the lives of inner-city and minority youth in this country. Instead, I choose to leverage every opportunity to invest in a positive identity for the next generation. It is our responsibility to share our stories to empower others.

Knowing now what I was unaware of then, I fight that much harder to guarantee I do not perpetuate the stereotypes placed on me but rather eradicate them by becoming everything they said I wouldn't be.

The realization that I am a target and a manufactured threat to those who have set out to destroy me since birth didn't set in until I was a teen. I remember having direct access to drugs, liquor, and guns by the age of thirteen but had to qualify for advanced academic and arts programs that were only offered in affluent school districts usually across town, 2 to 3 bus rides away. This is but one example of the subtle and subliminal ploys to eradicate black youth on an unrelenting systemic agenda.

Fully aware of what was orchestrated before I took my first step, I am intentional of leading by example, refraining from the urge to judge peers who may not be where I am in life or who may not demonstrate the level of wisdom or maturity as I do. I am sensitive to the plight that many of us didn't get to escape. I'm careful not to discount this generation based on the behaviors and mentalities imposed on them through media and pop culture. Instead, I take every chance to offer resources, information, and support to those who may not have had the same opportunities as I did. I'm learning to leverage every effort toward working to change the system, and not contribute to its destructive plan.

I want to encourage you this this mantra, and that is "where you start is not an indication of where you'll end up." You can have humble beginnings and legacy endings should you choose. It won't be easy, but it is possible. You can't control how things started, but once given the knowledge and opportunity, your narrative, journey, and legacy are up to you.

## The Complexity of MY Reflection

The toxic legacy of colorism has been a plague in the black community and to black culture long before I showed up in the winter of 1982; however, the pain of its prejudice certainly had an adverse effect on me. Now before you make assumptions, or jump to conclusions, I want to acknowledge as a light-skinned woman, I do not believe in "reverse colorism." What I do believe and what I have experienced however, is that light-skinned women are not immune to colorism.

My discomfort with being alienated and persecuted by my peers because of the perceptions that lighter-skinned women are more beautiful or more valued, and at times seen as weak, does not compare to the discrimination and disrespect darker-skinned women suffer. My intent is not to equate my experiences, but to share my perspective and to underline how shadeism affects our entire community.

Growing up "light skin" in a predominately black and Caribbean neighborhood made my siblings and I a target. As children of minority parents, we never believed we were "different," but the daily ridicule from our peers, mainly in school, suggested otherwise, eventually negatively influencing how we viewed ourselves. Me, I have the fairest skin of my mother's five children; and although I understood that I was a mixed-race child, I consciously self-identified as Black-American simply because of my upbringing, culture, and home life. I share this so you do not misunderstand my grievance and point-of-view; in no way am I claiming that the teasing and bullying my siblings and I experienced growing up could even compare to the inequalities that darker-complected men and women face in
this country.

Would you believe me if I told you all I ever wanted was a mahogany complexion? Well, it's true! I wanted nothing more than to be as beautiful and "sun-kissed" as some of my cousins, classmates, and neighbors. I hated being light skin! I was so dissatisfied with my lack of melanin that I would beg my mother to let me wear foundation in significantly darker hues, to which of course she
never allowed.

During summer I would intentionally stay in the sun for hours to achieve a deep tan only to cry hysterically when fall arrived each year fading my honey dipped complexion and once again revealing my naturally bright and pale pigment.

Only my parents and siblings knew how insecure I was about my complexion, and they understood why I hated going to school because of it. I cringed whenever I heard insulting labels like *"red bone," "high-yellow," "transparent,"* or *"Casper."* I was provoked to fight when I was accused of "thinking I was better than everyone else because I'm light skin," (which I did not think or believe by the way). And if I didn't end up in a fight, I was tortured with social isolation.

My classmates found it amusing to dare one another to slap me and see how red I could get, which was usually in my face. But what I hated most was the infamous phrase they repeated daily "here she comes, miss light bright, close to white!" I could feel myself shrinking from the mocking and taunting, pushing me deeper and deeper down a self-loathing spiral.

After a while, I intentionally wore black to school almost every day hoping the darker clothes would somehow offset my bright skin. But it never worked. It made things worse creating this weird hip hop goth look. Another flaw I was eventually teased for. I grew very resentful and began to do to others what was being done to me.

By the time I reached high school I purposely befriended light skin girls and isolated myself from my darker-skinned school mates. I believed surrounding myself with girls who looked like me would make me feel better about myself. And for a while it did but a part of me was still envious and bitter toward the bronzed beauties I so desperately wanted to look like.

As I got older my struggle with my complexion didn't improve or subside. Even after witnessing light-skinned and "exotic" women dominate music videos, movies, and television in the late 90's and early 2000's, I still fought to embrace my fair skin. Honestly, I still hated it. Point. Blank. Period. I was so unhappy with my complexion that I intentionally dated dark-skinned guys and promised myself that my future husband would be a "dark chocolate man" giving my children a better chance at having the complexion and melanin I always wanted.

When I got to college, I was old enough to wear make-up and my trouble with complexion and self-acceptance was more noticeable than ever. I was wearing make-up at least three shades darker than my natural complexion and it was painfully obvious. My face would resemble peanut butter and my hands, legs, and feet looked like white bread. It was a mess and a poor attempt at fixing on the outside what needed to be addressed on the inside.

I dragged the pain of my childhood experiences with skin tone into adulthood which perpetuated my insecurity and self-hate. I couldn't leave the house without make-up and felt the need to be "extra" to prove to everyone that I was black, despite what may have been assumed judging by my skin tone. I struggled to find a circle of friends that would reflect who I was, because honestly, I didn't know who I was.

I had no idea that the root of my self-doubt, and challenges connecting with other women all stemmed from my issues with complexion. My complexion to be exact. And I never felt safe enough to be vulnerable or honest about my issues. I was afraid of hearing responses like *"girl please, you lucky you have light skin!"* Or *"What are you complaining about? I wish I was your complexion!"* This fear of rejection forced me to deflect and blame my disposition and lack of confidence on other things. I worried about the discrediting and judgmental comments of disapproval for my audacious confessions.

For so long I thought it would be easier to just bury it and never speak on it, but it eventually interfered with other aspects of my life. The way I picked friends, dated, dressed, and behaved, were all a reflection of my insecurity. I didn't believe people when they complimented me and often assumed when people stared at me, they were talking about me. I never truly felt comfortable in my own skin. At times, a cute hairdo, or outfit would furnish temporary assurance, but it was never sustainable.

When the "Black Girl Magic" brand exploded on social media several years ago, I was hesitant to participate. I was afraid to post or recite this effectual expression of empowerment because I didn't feel it applied to me. I didn't feel qualified to be a melanin Queen or to promote my magic as a black woman. I know you're probably thinking, "wow, she's still dealing with this?" Yes! To this day, I struggle with my skin tone. Not as bad as I once did but I do have days that are worse than others. A significant part of my journey to wholeness, as referenced in my introduction, is to heal from this stigma that started in childhood and learn to love and accept who I am. To uncover what is unique and special about me. I affirm myself daily and am intentional in changing my perspective about the way
I look.

I am taking better care of my skin and not burying it under layers of foundation and make-up. I am embracing my fair skin and freckles. I am posting filter-free selfies on my social media and leaving the house in my natural face more frequently. I am learning to love the woman starring back at me in the mirror and learning to shine through my own reflection.

## Reclaiming the Gem Within

I read an article years ago, that said *"mediocrity is the root of all unhappiness."* The content writer went on to say that *"unhappiness sets in when you desire to be of service, but you have no idea what it is you have to contribute and why it matters."* This article described to the letter how I was feeling about my life. I knew I had a purpose and an assignment, but I had no clue what it was or how to uncover it.

The uncertainty left me feeling inadequate, and insignificant and eventually became unhappy with my life. The deficiencies, and loneliness I felt fueled my discontent even more as I subconsciously watched my normally jovial, and positive disposition dissipate under the weight of dissatisfaction and mediocrity.

I threw myself into my career, working non-stop to distract myself from this empty yet emotionally consuming feeling. I pretended to be pleased with my life and acted as if I had it altogether; even though the veneer I was using to hide my brokenness, and fear could be shattered with the least amount of force, exposing the real me. The bruised me. The conflicted me. I felt out of control, purposeless, and lost. I was strong to a fault, and skillfully disguised my pain under the faux persona of "an independent woman;" when deep down inside all I wanted was support and for someone to care.

I went on like this for years until the depression and stress began affecting my health. My diet and weight, skin, and mental well-being were all suffering and began to expose externally the affliction hindering me internally.

After a while, my unaddressed issues began to consume me. Comparable to physical wounds that go untreated, over time my symptoms were worsening and affecting other areas of my life. I was frustrated as a mom, disgruntled as an employee and unmotivated as a creative. I had no clue how to deal with my pain and was not in a conducive space to begin healing from it.

To no fault of my parents, my upbringing didn't equip me the tools necessary to manage my mental health or develop emotional intelligence. We were taught survival. My family would respond to trauma by reciting cliches like *"pray about," "toughen up,"* or *"that's just life."* Observing how my friends and family dealt with their pain, by not dealing with their pain, incited in me a long-term desire to change the pattern of emotional suffering, but I didn't know how or where to start. I continued to spiral and continued to lose myself in busyness and distracting activity.

Just a few months into the new year (2021), I had already compiled and independently published my second book, launched the Diamond Writers, rebranded my publishing boutique, completed my third degree, and received a significant promotion and raise
at work.

With all the positive changes, and accomplishments, you would assume I was happy right? WRONG! I couldn't even be proud of myself for my hard work; I didn't know how to celebrate "my wins" or enjoy the fruit of my labor. I literally felt nothing. I was happy for those connected to me in the process but didn't feel like I was worthy of the accolades. I pretended to be happy to appease those around me but deep down inside I still felt dispirited.

Amid the aforementioned, I met a man, an amazing man, and early into the relationship he noticed my insatiable need to work or to stay "busy," my excessive shopping and frequent crying. These were all unhealthy coping mechanisms that I had depended on and used as a crutch to survive the day to day.

One day he sat me down to talk, and in the most nonthreatening and nonjudgmental way, he asked if he could teach me meditation and breathing exercises to replace some of the unhealthy habits I had been using to cope. In full transparency, I was not at all ready to deal with my mess; I had gotten comfortable in this space and so I was dejectedly resistant.

My perspective and vision were clouded by my own discontent, so it was difficult for me to see the benefits of implementing these small lifestyle changes. And I honestly didn't believe they would even help me. But he was persistent and committed to aiding me in my healing.

Finally, I gave in and began to practice what he taught me. I began my days with guided meditation and positive affirmations. I started to make healthier food choices and paid closer attention to my physical and mental health. I resisted the urge to scroll on social media for hours or to sit and watch mindless television. Instead, I returned to my passion for reading and journaling, two outlets I had forfeited after becoming inundated with managing my depression, and faux identity.

Journaling helped me to release pinned up anger and reduced my anxiety. It allowed me to record my feelings and helped me to identify patterns and trends in my behavior and helped me to avoid certain triggers. The more I nurtured my mind and spirit, the clearer I could see myself. My problems were magnified, and not in a way that would prompt pain, but in an exposing way to provoke action. These gradual changes helped me to uncover deeply rooted pain from my past; mistakes, and the consequences of poor decisions that I had subconsciously buried. This unhealthy avoidance was what developed my self-destructive behavior.

It is clear to me now that the smallest effort toward change can improve your life. I am very much still early in my journey, with so much more work ahead of me, but it feels good to look back and reflect on my progress thus far. My perspective, and thoughts toward myself and my life are enhancing daily. I'm no longer afraid to be vulnerable, to admit I need help or that I'm feeling unsure. I don't try to solve every problem on my own, and I'm strong enough to admit fault and apologize. I'm nurturing and reconciling the relationships and friendships that serve me and removing those that don't. I am excited about my future and the possibility of enjoying it from a healthy and authentic place.

I don't hate who I was nor who I've been pretending to be, but I am glad I don't have to be her anymore. I am learning how to overcome circumstances, no longer being defeated by them. I'm taking my power back by reclaiming my identity and improving my overall quality of life one purpose driven day at a time. I feel liberated, not lucky; blessed, not bitter. I embrace this season and am proud of my growth and maturity.

If you can truly look at yourself and confirm you are genuinely who you're supposed to be, then keep living, Sis! But if you know, who you've been and who you are is not the real you, then I'd like to offer you this advice:

- **Heal!** Make your healing a priority. It's never apparent to us at the time, but our emotional wounds must be healed and cared for in the same way, and with the same sense of urgency as our physical wounds are. We have the propensity to treat physical trauma within minutes of the injury but will wait years before we even look at the emotional wounds besetting us. We are not as aggressive in the treatment and usually won't invest the same amount of time in healing. Take accountability and be reminded that you are responsible for your healing. It's on you to seek counseling, read books, pray, cry, or journal. Your friends, family, clergy and/or trained professionals can assist, and support you, but the work must come from you.

- Swallow your pride, release your ego, and surrender your will; doing so does not make you weak, it makes you wise. Too often we forfeit great relationships, and opportunities because we are too stubborn, or too proud to admit we were wrong, or show vulnerability. Understand that there is value in vulnerability, and that, without it, there is no growth, no healing, and no change.

- Do the work. Introspective work, shadow work, whatever you desire to call it, if you put in the work, it will lead you down a path of deeper healing, self-awareness, and transformation. Give yourself grace and room to hurt as you heal. This process can be just as painful as the injury, but I promise you'll come out stronger.

- Don't rush the process; trust the process. It wasn't until 2021 that I finally made myself, my healing, and my happiness a priority. This is not to say that I neglect my responsibilities or ignore commitments. It simply means that among my priorities, I am the priority, I top the list! You can't pour into others what you don't give to yourself first. You cannot pour from an empty cup. Make it a habit to refill and replenish your cup first and then pour into others from your overflow. Even the airlines teach you to secure your mask first before assisting others. You are no good to anyone if you are not first good to yourself.

- Lastly, believe you are worth every effort and worthy of a fulfilling, and purpose-driven life. You attract what you believe you deserve, so dwell on good things, hopeful things, healthy things. Vibrate higher daily and be intentional in your actions, thoughts, and connections. Be grateful for what you have as you pursue what you want, and you'll always have something to look forward to.

## Comfortable in Chaos

Growing up I took a city bus to school and just about every day exchanged energy with disgruntled bus drivers, angry commuters, and rowdy students. Once I arrived on Jamaica Avenue (Sutphin & Archer to be exact) I had to walk several blocks to my high school, passing street vendors, gypsy cab drivers, drunks, homeless people, street pharmacists and their clientele. Being hit on during my route to school wasn't an uncommon occurrence either.

Arriving at school I had to walk through metal detectors and check-in at identification turnstiles but not before witnessing gang rivals square up in front of the school over territory beef or just mutual dislike.

As an adult I think back and question how the hell I was able to manage such mental stress, and chaos in such toxic environments and still find the focus to lock into coursework and curriculum each day. How did I mentally transition from survival to learning in a matter of minutes every morning? I experienced and endured more drama, and danger before first period than most will in their lifetime. There was no down time between arriving at school and starting my first class of the day to reset.

This type of environment had become my "norm" and any setting or atmosphere that wasn't steeped in confusion or disorder made me uncomfortable. After my parents' divorce, my home life resembled my morning commute and school backdrop. My entire life revolved around organized and routine chaos.

My dependency on chaos to feel normal was a very unhealthy addiction that I had to work hard to break and unlearn. As I highlighted earlier in my chapter, this healing process takes work. It takes intention, and consistency. It takes patience, and accountability to establish a sense of normalcy. If you're like me and "thrive" or feel most comfortable in a chaotic environment, I want to share a few tips and best practices that are helping me to reverse my reliance on chaotic patterns:

- Create a routine that centers you and energizes you. Create a space that supports you and what you want to accomplish or achieve in your day. I learned years ago that a messy or cluttered room, home, car, or other living space is an external representation of what's going on internally. Creating a space that is clean, organized, and structured will cultivate a conducive environment for your healing and growth.

- Increase your vibrational awareness and adjust your perspective. Being aware of your vibrational levels will improve what and who you attract. If you're like me, when I operated in a "chaos dependent state of mind" it showed up in multiple areas of my life. My finances and spending habits, my work habits, and my relationships. My prior relationships were toxic, consistent fighting, and lacked trust and respect. It was chaotic and yet they all lasted for several years. This was again, my chaos dependency manifesting in my energy and vibe. Changing your vibration will support you in modifying your perspective and severing your addiction to chaos.

- Stop allowing the news or social media to claim your early morning attention. The world we live in is chaotic, social media is chaotic, so allowing these mediums to influence the first thing you observe and absorb is counterproductive to breaking the cycle of chaos dependency. You must start your day the way you want to experience and end your day. Consider starting your day with a guided meditation, affirmations, a walk, prayer, reading or journaling. Whatever you choose, make sure it has a positive influence on your mind and energy. If you must, wake up an extra thirty minutes earlier every day to ensure you get the first fruits of your day. A concentrated focus will contribute to a higher vibration.

## Crown Her

In my humble opinion, there is a habitual misuse and diluted definition of what and who a Queen is. And although I am not the authority on the use or application of the noun, I do feel qualified to enlighten you on what I believe a "Queen" is (or is not).

A Queen is not just a female ruler of an independent state, or the most powerful chess piece; she's not just a high-value face card in a suit or deck, nor is she merely the "mother of most" in her colony or beehive. A Queen is one of divine status, caliber, and nature. She is a high-quality woman, not a bad bitch. She demonstrates "royal behavior" and is governed by integrity, decorum, and compassion. She is vulnerable, empathetic, and kind. She is intellectually, emotionally, spiritually, and energetically balanced, and doesn't allow her insecurities or faults to go unaddressed, nor does she allow them to invalidate her.

She is far from perfect, but her dignity and self-esteem are embodied in the way she walks, talks, dresses, and acts. She doesn't allow the judgments or comments of others to disrupt the way she lives her life, nor does she surrender to her own negative self-talk.

Her invisible crown adorns her head like an ornament of confidence and inherent worth. Not to be mistaken for arrogant, she is free of the common propensity to seek approval or validation from social media or from random men. The attention she gets does not result from a pretentious façade or an inflated view of self, but rather from her radiance and magnetic feminine energy.

A Queen is a vibe, an unparalleled energetic force in female form.

Queenship is so much more than a desirable and attractive label. It is a responsibility, a significant and authoritative disposition. It is a commitment to not only honor yourself but to support, and uplift others under the same diadem. To be mindful of your words, considerate of your actions and thoughtful about your intentions.

To reach back to the generation of young Queens behind you, not to judge what you may not understand about them, but to speak life and purpose that would inspire them. Reaching out to those next to you, allowing them to lean on you, learn from you and lead with you. And finally reaching ahead to the Queens before you; to those whose legacies we stand on, benefit from, and carry on.

A Queen is one that has dealt with her past, embraces the present and plans for her future. She is an example of triumph, perseverance, and resilience. She is an attitude, an energy, an inspiration, and an influencer.

Know that you are a Queen, capable of anything, and unstoppable by nothing. You are a light, a force and creator. Your past does not define you, who you used to be cannot hinder you. You have the power to redirect your life and rewrite the narrative if you
so choose.

I hope after reading this chapter, you are inspired to use your voice. Leverage your power. And write your story!

# Recovery After Loss

## Chelle Mack

In 2013, I was newly married, working full-time in a great paying job in Lower Manhattan, serving in ministry, caring for our teenage daughter and providing support in whatever way I could to our family and close friends. I had overextended myself and was under a lot of stress.

I had to re-evaluate my priorities to assess what was important. While at work one day, I nearly passed out because of the stress I was under. After I talked with my husband about the matter, we prayed. I resigned from my full-time position to take a less strenuous position. I learned that peace and a peaceful work environment were more important than money.

The new position I accepted was an office sales position in Midtown NY. I would walk around my assigned territory and sell office supplies to companies in the region.

Three months into the position, I became seriously ill. I was experiencing sharp pains in my body. I had never experienced pain like this before. It was not cramps, I was not spotting, it felt as though I was being stabbed. I tried to self-medicate, thinking

that I may have walked too much that day. I was wrong and was taken to the ER
for treatment.

The medical staff ran tests and later discovered that I had a cyst on my kidney and was also a few weeks pregnant. Wait... what?

I needed to see a series of specialists to identify what the best treatment plan for my conditions were. I was beyond scared to say the least. All I could think was, Cyst... what kind of cyst(s)? Is this cancerous? What will happen to my teenage daughter? And
a newborn?

## We're Having a Baby

My husband and I wanted a son. Prior to getting married, we had talked about having kids together. We talked about the number of kids we wanted and their gender (as if we have control over this, lol). Now, we were having a baby!

My husband and I talked about every detail we could think of. I don't think I thought about the potential complications that I could face during the pregnancy. But I did believe that God would keep His promise to me and grant us our heart's desire, despite our current circumstances.

During the fifth month of my pregnancy, I began to experience severe back pain and spotting. By this time, I was no longer working as I needed to take things slow. I was not placedon bedrest by my doctor; however, she was monitoring my condition closely.

One day while visiting my parents, I felt as though I needed to lay down. So, my mom recommended that I get some rest. A few hours later, I was rushed to the ER because I was spotting and experiencing labor pains. Unfortunately, the hospital I was taken to did not have a labor and delivery unit.

The medical team did the best that they could do until I could be transferred to another hospital that specialized in the care we needed. While there, I could see the sympathy in the eyes of the nurse who cared for me. She knew something I did not know and did not want to tell me. She knew I was about to experience my first miscarriage.

## Our Son is Born

Early the next morning, I was transferred to a specialty hospital by an ambulance and my husband followed in a separate car. The medical team did their best to make me as comfortable as possible. I was taken to the labor and delivery unit. I was scared, even though I knew that God was with me.

I went into labor shortly after I arrived in my room. Our baby was born. However, this was a stillborn birth. Our son died during the delivery, on July 15th, 2013.

Later that day, I was moved into a peaceful room with calla lilies on the wall. Calla lilies were my favorite flower. I knew that God was with us, even though we had just experienced this great loss. Afterall, God understood better than anyone. His son, Jesus, died on the cross for the sins of the world. Although I knew that God was with us and that He understood, it was still a challenge to deal with my emotions and heartbreak.

## Fighting For My Life

After I was discharged the first time, I did not heal as quickly as the doctors had planned. My health took a turn for the worse. I had an infection and was experiencing what felt like labor pains.

The medical staff working this day were more interested in building their resumés than helping me as a patient. They wanted to conduct a hysterectomy. They did not know anything about me. They did not see me as a woman who was grieving the loss of her son. It felt as if no one saw me, or saw the pain that I was in. I was told that I needed a procedure that would take away any future chance of me having more children.

What about the dreams my husband and I shared? What about my heart?

This doctor had no bedside manner. I decided to speak up for myself, kicked her out of the room and told her that she did not have permission to touch me. I called for the patient advocate and filed a formal complaint.

After asserting myself, we were able to learn the cause of my pain. It was uterine fibroids and now they were degenerating/dying. The doctor explained the next steps towards my recovery would require that I go into labor (again) and deliver the degenerating fibroids.

We did not make it to that stage in my care plan. I became extremely ill. The medical team's solution was that I needed to have an emergency myomectomy. I was quickly taken to another room to be prepared for surgery in the hope that it would save my life. This room looked nothing like the first. This room was unwelcoming, dark and cold.

We did not know if I was going to make it this time around. My husband was not in agreement with this surgical procedure. He wanted me to wait until he arrived at the hospital so that he could ask questions. Unfortunately, the situation was dire, and it couldn't wait. I had been prepared for a surgery that he knew nothing about, and I could see the hurt in his eyes. I asked for his forgiveness as I was taken into surgery.

I did my best to make the surgeon promise not to perform a hysterectomy on me. As the anesthesia kicked in, I made peace with God and relinquished my need to be in control.

The surgery was a success. Glory to God in the highest, I am still here by the grace of God! The doctors that were involved with my care plan were in complete shock when I walked out of the hospital on that day in September. It was a miracle.

## Now the Real Work Begins...

I began seeing a mental health therapist to help me process my thoughts and emotions. She was not a Christian; she was someone that God used to help me face and walk through the trauma I had experienced. I needed someone who could guide me through the pain in a healthy and structured way. I met with her weekly. At first, I was a little apprehensive, however, I began to put my walls down after the fourth counseling session. My therapist would assign exercises to help me through my pain.

One of the assignments I was given was to give a name to our baby and to have a memorial in his memory. My husband and I decided on the name Stephen.

With each session, I got stronger and learned how to express how I was feeling in a healthier way.

In my counseling sessions, I learned:

- It was okay to be angry.

- It was okay to feel how I was feeling.

- It was not my fault that I miscarried.

- It was okay to be sad.

- It was okay to cry uncontrollably—my heart was broken.

- Depression was a part of my grieving process; however, I could not stay there.

- I did not have to be strong or put on a front.

- Everyone does not know what to say to bring comfort to you. Forgive them anyway.

My son, Stephen (smile) came into this world to make a difference in our family. He fulfilled his purpose here on Earth and I look forward to seeing him again.

My God is a Promise Keeper!

God answered our prayers! A year later, the cyst that I had on my kidney was surgically removed. No cancer detected. Three years later, we became the proud parents of a beautiful son.

## The Crown Assist

If you are experiencing/have experienced this type of grief, I want to encourage you to:

- Know that support is a necessary part of your recovery (such as licensed mental health professional and support groups).

- Accept the fact that sometimes there are things completely out of your control.

- Seek wise counsel from someone outside your immediate circle.

- Understand that sadness is natural and real.

- Insist on having someone advocate for you and your health in the hospital.

- Talk about the miscarriage with your spouse/partner. They are hurting too. It will help you both heal.

The points above and prayer were vital for my recovery and healing. I pray that you are encouraged to take the necessary steps needed for your healing.

# The Breakup Wake Up

## Tiffany R Mathias

I have always been the type of person to seek fulfillment in everything I do. I have never felt the need to waste time and energy if I'm only going to half-ass something. I was also raised to have pride in what I do. I was told that no matter what I decided to do in life, the effort I put forth to achieve my outcome better result in something I was proud to put my name on.

My husband would say that created a "good soldier work ethic." We had many heated arguments about that. In hindsight, I cannot necessarily argue with him anymore on that point. That was exactly my attitude. I was the type of employee every leader wanted on their team. I came in early, I stayed late. I worked through my lunches (if I took them at all). I brought my work home with me. I answered calls from work on my day off. I would feel guilty about calling out and utilizing justly earned paid time off.

I subsequently learned the issue with this type of devotion and mindset. For a long time, I was dedicating myself and giving my best efforts to an unhealthy, one-sided relationship. Now, the funny thing is, when we think about relationships, we generally think of our connections and engagements with people. Very rarely do we think of our connections and ties to the other two nouns: places and things.

It was not so long ago that I realized I was in a toxic relationship with my career. Like most toxic relationships, I am not exactly sure when the relationship actually soured. I cannot pinpoint for you the moment when I no longer felt happy or excited about going to work. I cannot remember the last time I left work and felt complete. Many times, I walked out the building and was dreadfully counting down the hours until I was required to return.

I know one thing for sure. One particular morning, I was getting ready for work and just as I finished getting dressed and did my final assessment before walking out the door, I looked at myself in the bathroom mirror and cried.

Staring back at me was a sullen face with heavily bagged eyes. My shoulders were slumped, and my jaw was clenched tightly. My appearance did not resemble that of a successful woman headed for a days' work. The reflection peering back at me resembled that of a person heading to court on verdict day. My sentence? Twenty years to life of hard labor.

Now do not get me twisted. I did not always feel like this, and the truth is, my circumstances were not all my employer's fault, either. You see, just like in a toxic romantic relationship, there were two parties involved.

There used to be a time when I enjoyed my work. I looked forward to going into my workplace. I liked my coworkers. I had a great team working for me. I found pride in my career. Many times, I actually spoke about my job at career fairs. I gave presentations on what a typical day looked like for me. I could speak on the necessary educational requirements and training. I could even converse with people who showed interest in my field and let them know if I thought they would be successful or not.

At this time, I will let you know that I will not tell you what field my career was in. That tidbit of information is irrelevant to this story. If I were referring to a person, identifying them by name would be insignificant. Revealing the person by his/her name, would not change my situation. As a matter of fact, in a scenario like that, more times than not, a pseudonym is used to protect those involved. It does not matter if the person's name is John, Sue, Kesha, or Jamal. Therefore, it is insignificant for me to reveal if I was a lawyer, a banker, a salesperson, or a flight attendant. The important factor for you to know is that the career no longer served my purpose. As it so happens, it drained me physically, emotionally, and spiritually.

Returning to that day in the bathroom, I thought about who I was in that moment. The person I was 20-odd years ago was not who looked back at me in the mirror. The happy-go-lucky, optimistic, "make the best of things" person who had been full of ideas was gone. Standing before me was a woman who was jaded, angry, lackluster and downright miserable.

Now we know what they say about misery. She loves company. Therefore, in spite of my best efforts, there were times my misery took ahold of my workday, and I made every and any one I came into contact with miserable. It was not pleasant working with me or for me, for that matter.

Side note: If you are reading this book, and my foolishness impacted you, I humbly apologize to you for my actions and attitude, as well as for the bearing they had on you. You did not deserve that. I should have been better. Done better.

Here is the funniest, and, I would say, the most ironic thing about my "breakup" with my career: I was not the one who ended the relationship! While I was in my corner, licking my wounds, plotting my escape, I did not execute my plan in enough time. After more than three years of saying I was going to leave and start anew, I received my walking papers from my employer.

It was the utmost surreal thing that had ever happened to me. I am certain that I will never forget that day as long as I live. It is permanently etched in my memory right next to the birth of my children and in between my wedding day and my father joining the ancestors, because it was a life altering moment that would reshape me going forward.

My workday had started as it typically did. There was a conference call scheduled for later in the afternoon, but those were not out of the ordinary.

I hated those calls. For me, they were full of people reading scripts and regurgitating stats and metrics. All things I could read and analyze on my own time in an email.

As the time approached, my coworkers and I gathered in our manager's office for the call. I brought a snack and something to drink in with me. I even had some paperwork that required my attention. I thought to myself, *If I am going to be sitting still for the time being, I might as well make it productive.* There goes that "good solider" thing again. Multitasking like I was the newest model of the Tiffany 2.0.

The call started with the usual role call and salutations. Then it quickly turned serious. As stats and figures were recited from the script, I half listened, ate my snack and tended to my paperwork. About 30 minutes into the call, something was said that caught my full attention. The word was *realignment.*

I put my pencil down and gave the office phone my full attention. More facts and figures were spewed, then the call ended with the facilitator stating immediately following the call, individual meetings would happen with each person that was on the call as well as their direct manager.

My stomach sank. I looked around the room at my coworkers. Everyone seemed stuck in the same moment I was. A herd of deer caught in headlights. We all knew what this meant, but no one
said anything.

*Question:* have you ever attended a program orientation and been told, "Look to your left, now look to your right. One of these people will not make it to the end?" Well, that is exactly what was happening. Eyeballs darted around the room, trying to figure out just who was going to be impacted by this *realignment.*

I knew. Spirit told me. But Spirit also told me to stay calm and I heard my father's voice say, "It's okay. You're going to be alright."

One by one, we exited the office and were told by our manager the order he would see us in. I was last. I guzzled my water, gathered up the rest of my uneaten snack, and paperwork, then headed for my office to await my turn.

When I was called in, I tried to make it easy for him. I could tell by the look on his face that I was the one being let go. Here I was, the one getting the axe, and I was trying to ease the tension in the room. (Salute. "Aye, Aye Captain.")

Once I sat down, my manager spoke. Words came out his mouth, but my ears stopped listening and my brain refused to make sense of what he was saying. Eventually, he handed me a stack of papers I had not noticed sitting by his hands. He told me to read and review the entire document carefully. He let me know that this was not his decision and it pained him to have to deliver this news.

I felt his pain. I would not have wanted to be in his shoes. I had worked as this man's right hand for six years. We had worked closely together, and I could finish his sentences. At times I did, jokingly, just to annoy him. We had a very casual and close relationship. He knew my children and would ask about them often.

As our meeting continued, I could see the discomfort in his demeanor. He was having a difficult time saying what he had to, and I had a hard time listening. He finally ended our conversation by stating he appreciated all the years I had spent working for him, reiterated the fact that my presence would be missed and offered partnership as I searched out my new endeavors.

I just nodded my head repeatedly. I did not trust my voice. I knew it would fail me. I could feel a lump in my throat the size of a grapefruit forming. I knew that if I did not get out of that office soon, I would be crying in front of this man. I stood up, took my severance notice, and walked out.

I felt the tears burning to fall from my swollen eyes. I tried to make sense of it all. In 45 minutes, my life was changed forever. I asked for some time, explaining that I need some fresh air and to go walk it off. I was working late that night, and all I kept thinking was, *I need to clear my head so that I can finish out my day.*

*What!?* Who does that? As my world was flipped and turned on its axis, all I could manage to think about was the final impressions I was going to leave behind.

I wanted to go grab my belongings and flip the place off. I needed to call my husband. I needed the person who sees the silver lining in everything to find the one in this situation. But first, I needed to scream at the top of my lungs about just how unfair and unjust life was. I wanted to call my girlfriends so they could play good angel/bad devil and crack jokes at me so I could laugh to keep from crying. That night dragged on forever. I stayed in my office most of that night with the lights off and my feet up on the desk. *Why not?* I thought. *What are they going to do, fire me?*

While I was advised by my family and friends to pack my shit and get out of there right away, I decided that I was going to retain my dignity and professionalism. Part of my package required me to finish out the month. I had a definitive end date and so I just needed to make the best of it.

Though I was not leaving on my terms, I decided that when I walked out of my workplace for the last time, I was going to do it with my head held high and theme music playing. (Insert finger snaps.)

I spent the next few weeks on autopilot. I showed up for work every day that I was scheduled and did my job. Oh! And to add insult to injury, I was asked to give crash courses in everything I did. Yup. I had to teach those still with jobs how to do my job. With my position being eliminated, that meant my coworkers would have to step up to the plate and take on added responsibilities.

A devious part of me wanted to teach them everything incorrectly and ass-backwards. Though my inner Petty Betty was ready to act up, I thought better. What would all that prove, other than that I was immature, trivial and vindictive?

Like a good soldier, I taught them the most efficient ways to get things done. I also had some tough conversations with my team. Many of them had spent their entire tenure with the company working directly for me, and now they were losing their leader. This was not going to be easy for them. There were some who were loyal to a fault and started talking about quitting and transferring to other locations because they did not want to work for the organization any longer. I could not let that happen.

In the end, my last weeks at that job revealed to me something that I had long since denied: I did have power in my influence. I had built something remarkable with that team. They were my work family, and I was going to miss them.

I recall having a conversation with one particular employee who worked in a different department. This young lady was in tears at the news she was hearing. I let her have her moment and when she was done, I had her wipe her eyes and hugged her. I reassured her that I was going to be okay. I let her know that all this meant was that my work here was done, and it was time for me to move on.

Lastly, I told her that I could not allow her to transfer the feelings of sadness she was experiencing onto me. I believe our emotions and internal energies are fluid and can be passed from one person to the next. I needed this young lady to be okay because I did not want the negative or low vibrational energy of her sadness to affect others or myself. I believed I was going to be okay but I did not want my faith in myself to be shaken by someone else's perceptions.

As I prepared for my final departure, I knew all eyes were on me. The pressure mounted day by day, week by week as I felt some people were waiting for me to crack and give in to the pressures of my circumstance.

The additional weight of being a minority woman did not help either. As a woman, and as a minority woman, there are certain unwritten rules I had to contend with. When there are not that many of us in the room, we become the litmus strip by which some people gauge *all* of us. Therefore, my actions, reactions and behaviors could potentially be damaging to the image of all professional women of color if I did not carry myself in the utmost and proper manner. That is why I had to keep my petty streak under control.

I stayed the course and dug deeper into my roots. This resulted in my ability to stay grounded during this time of uncertainty. Besides, I had no reason to be sad or disappointed in my circumstances, other than the fact that this company had beat me to the punch.

The only reason for my dismay was my injured pride. Yes, my ego was badly bruised. I was now in a situation where the rumor mill was starting to spin and the whispers behind my back and closed doors were that I had failed to meet expectations and was being terminated for my performance. However, never in my professional experience has someone who has failed company expectations and been given a termination notice been allotted 20 days' notice to vacate their position.

So, I had to let the rumors fly and stand in my truth. That truth was, my organization had shareholders and a board of directors they answered to and after the global pandemic known as COVID-19 wreaked havoc on the economy, this organization needed to turn a profit in the 2021 fiscal year. The quickest and most common way to make that happen is through layoffs and budget cuts.

As I said earlier, I am not exactly sure when I no longer felt fulfilled by my career. I was already on a new career path and building my personal brand. My career goals and aspirations were changing. I knew in my soul that this situation had been provided to me as an opportunity to step outside my comfort zone and was a chance to grow beyond my current self.

Opportunities for growth and self-revolution do not come at time's convenience. Growth can be quite uncomfortable and even painful at times. New prospects in life come when we least suspect they will. They manifest when we are standing at a crossroad with choices of great consequence to make.

I was standing, ready to take the path I knew was the safest. They arrived, postage due and no time to misstep. Stepping out onto faith in myself and my ability to sink or swim was gut wrenching.

Increasing my mindfulness, I had to learn to let go of things quicker. I had to purge myself of people, places and things that disrupted my energy and stifled my creative flow.

I was once told that in order to figure this out, I needed to ask myself this question, "Will this matter to me next week?"

Exploring this train of thought even further, I started to shorten this scale even more. I changed the word "week" and replaced it with "day," then "hour." Once I was able to truthfully answer those questions, I started feeling better, lighter, even. I was free from unnecessary burdens that only I was carrying. I was no longer tied to the people, places or things that held me back from my greatness.

We all have it in us to manifest our greatness. Like any other muscle in our bodies, our growth muscle has to exercise and be worked out often. It is not easy, and results will not be seen immediately.

At first, it can feel overwhelming. Voices from those around you, some with your best interest at heart, others probably not, will play over and over in your head. You have to learn how to filter through those and sort out which is which.

Declare your purpose. Start to plan. Carry a journal or notebook. Write down everything. Preparation is key. Set goals, both long and short term, and prioritize them. Do your research and figure out what is needed for you to achieve your new goals. This is you laying out your game plan.

Read your goal list daily. Add new objectives to your list that will continue to build towards your goals. Cross off those items that no longer align with your plans as they start to form. Celebrate your victories and analyze your defeats. Then start over again.

Just like when we are no longer in those toxic relationships with people, we go through periods of self-assessment when we end toxic relationships with the workplace. We seek out answers in attempts to figure out where we went wrong and look for all the things we could have done differently. This is natural and just part of the process.

I would also say that we look to take on more blame than need be. We are our own harshest critics. I tell myself, *Do not over analyze this. Just seek answers in what you have control over. Those are the only aspects you can change.*

Since the conclusion of my employment with that organization, I have spent my time focusing on my family. I have reprioritized my next career moves and forged forward with my plans to open my own businesses. I have taken on more roles and responsibilities in partnership with some of my associates in their own endeavors.

I no longer feel the heavy burden of dread of working for an organization that claims to support a healthy work/life balance and cares about its employees, while its requirements speak to the
exact opposite.

Every day, I am free to be me and work on me. All the same efforts and energy that I put into being a good soldier and making sure the organizations I was employed by made their bottom-line goals, I put into myself instead. I found the value in myself and refuse to allow another corporation to use me and cause me to lose seeing the value in me.

Finding my own purpose and striving towards my own goals changed my outlook on other facets of my life. In a domino effect, one by one, I changed for the better and I am happier for it. That conference call forced me out of my comfort zone and ended up being the best thing that could have happened in my professional life.

# Her Power

# All your Mosaic Self

## Kris J

They say the eyes are the windows to the soul...

So, there I was, sitting in Haiti, and watching how people were staring at me. Needless to say, I was nervous as fuck. They were all looking at me intensely and I was looking right back. But the moment our eyes locked, I looked away as if to say, "No, please don't stare at me."

But then I remembered I had mirror sunglasses on. It instantly boosted my confidence because I started to feel like a child with superhero invisibility goggles on. I smiled and now they looked away. Almost as if they could tell I had turned my superpower on. I was laughing on the inside because I was confused as to why I was afraid of them staring in the first place.

You are gorgeous, girl! They are staring at you because they can't believe how amazing you are. There I was, afraid to lock eyes with a person for fear that they may actually see that I didn't feel as gorgeous as they thought I was. Afraid that they would see the insecurities behind my eyes and expose them for the world to see.

To see. The proper definition is to view something (person/place/thing) in its authentic form with your eyes. You can't see anything without your eyes, third eye or otherwise (and nothing against prophets or the spirituals, let's just stay literal for this one point). Your eyes are important but also sensitive transmissions of frequencies. They are a safe.

You ever heard someone say, "There is a story behind your eyes." Because there is so much pain, power and peace behind your eyes that one can almost read the story which is your soul. It's almost as if life's experiences are made up of tiny pieces of fragile glass that all come together to make a beautiful yet fragile mosaic structure.

Typically, a mosaic statue of such importance would be displayed in a museum, and a museum would never have fragile items on display without any form of protection. However sometimes they are a little too protective, shielding not only from the outside world but from spectators alike.

While I can appreciate our need for protection, figuratively, our souls are fearfully hiding behind our eyes. Often, we use our inability to connect eyes for any extended amount of time as a shield meant to shelter, but actually, it only highlights our insecurities. Most of us avoid direct eye contact, falsely thinking we are protecting our souls (and ourselves) by not allowing anyone to see them, but that is the furthest from the truth. We are actually doing ourselves and society
a great disservice by not allowing our spirits to shine to their
fullest potential.

You ever see a photo of someone and say, "Man, this picture makes me feel like he is staring into my soul"? (I'm totally imagining Kofi from Queen Sugar but let me get back on topic.)

The idea of them staring into your soul and you feeling nervous or anxious is actually your subconscious knocking on your soul's window. It's saying, "Hey, have you seen you? You're fucking amazing." Why are we hiding from the world?

It brings me back to that museum. When we think about those people in our lives who look at us with those "soul snatching eyes," they have the same mosaic life statue I'm describing. But whether they are an actor, entertainer, teacher, mechanic, hairstylist, etc., those individuals are no longer inside of the museum. They are outside!

As any amateur photographer, I believe sunlight is the best light. Who wouldn't want to be viewed in the best light possible? You know it's all about those angles. Quick shot out to the sun for its many healing properties and just being abundantly awesome. The point is that when you are outside, the world gets to see you. All the imperfections, the fragility, the beauty, the strength and the glory. I don't know any indoor light that can capture all of that.

Additionally, another bonus to being outside with all your mosaic self is that you get to be free, not confined to the walls of the museum or, in this case, the idealism of other's opinions.

If we are being honest with ourselves, the opinions of others control so much of our actions, whether we want to admit it or not. Oftentimes we hesitate in life for fear that we may not be good enough. That goes for whatever your version of "good enough" is. You are not obligated to live up to someone else's idea of "doing good." Your only job is to just simply be. Embrace who the Most High created you to be. Stop living your life trapped in the museum, only able to look out the windows of your eyes. Come outside!

It's shiny out here. There's free space, fresh air and nature (which is a natural dopamine boost). You know that feeling you get when the weather finally breaks from winter? Spring shows up and you can't wait to step outside with your freshly manicured toes, while allowing the sun to pleasantly beam on your face. You find yourself excited to go for a walk simply because everything in nature seems to be alive and happy.

Well, I want your spirit to have that type of joy each day. Wear that dress that makes you smile when you put it on, no bother if you may be overdressed at Target. Do it because it feels good to you.

Go outside, spin around on the grass in the front yard. Who cares what the neighbors think? Doesn't it feel amazing to let the sun beam directly on you without the filter of the window screen?

Quick question, what happens when the sun hits the side of a mosaic wall? It reflects the light!

Being outside and letting the sun beam directly on you allows you to shine for others to see from their windows. Similar to my mirrored sunglasses, you are mirroring their souls for them to see. I believe that if you do the inner work, shaking up souls with your eyes or even locking eyes with others will no longer scare you. It will empower you!

Think back to a time when you were younger, and you absolutely loved to play outside with your favorite friends. But what happened if you or one your friends got in trouble? Your mom would say, "You're not going outside to play today." But you and your friends quickly devised a plan (from the window of course) to sweet talk her into changing her mind so you could be set free. Surprisingly, it worked! Your mom granted you freedom. Then you were in your favorite place... outside!

Let's just take a moment and think about how good it felt. You felt like you were magical. Like you had figured out a way to crack the code to the parental punishment prison. You felt as though you were sitting on top of the world. Happiness in its truest form for what you knew about life as a kid.

Now, what if we could tap into that child-like joy every day? A little later in this next section, we will discuss some simple steps you can take to move all your mosaic self out of the museum and stand outside for the world to see.

What if we saw ourselves for exactly the way the world views us? Why are we afraid to be as fabulous as they tell us we are? Do we fear that it would be impolite to be too amazing?

Well, I'll tell you, I have never been around a dope souled person and thought, "Oh no, they are too amazing, lemme runaway!"

If Beyonce was in the room and you were the chief of the Beyhive, you would never say to her, "Thank you, Beyonce, but I have had enough of your presence." Watching the clock would be the furthest thing from your mind. In fact, one would probably be pondering how to manipulate the physics of time in an effort to have more time with her. I am certain celebrities have to put time limits on meet and greets for this very reason. Folk just can't get enough of a good thing.

While Beyonce is phenomenal in so many ways, even the biggest fan can't have full access to the fullness of "she." Again, this is for demonstration purposes only. Assuming Mrs. Carter is a mosaic statue delicately placed in a viewing garden, she still has the ability to only allow us access to certain parts of herself. She does this through entertainment and expressing herself very vibrantly.

Like any statue sitting on the lawn. The sun rises on one side, then sets on the opposite. When it shines on the front, a shadow is cast in the back. Where do you think shadow work comes from?

Using Beyonce as an example again, just because she is outside does not make her exempt from shadow work. We just don't get to see all of her because she can choose what angle to stand at whatever part of the day, wherever the sun is in the sky to control the shadows cast.

Your being outside for the world to see doesn't mean you have to give your full self to the world. You are allowed to design the type of garden you want to sit in. How many visitors you allow inside or deny access to is up to you. You are even in charge of what type of security walls (or boundaries) you would like to have up, for that matter.

Of course, there will always be spectators walking by and wondering whatever it is that spectators wonder. But your job isn't to accommodate their thoughts. Your job is to utilize the sun's energy to enhance or highlight your God-given talents and purposes for the advancement of not only your life's journey, but also for your community. Allowing the sun to reflect through you undoubtably makes other's lives brighter, simply by you existing.

Have you ever stood next to an old radio with one of the extendable antennas? The signal sounds amazing while you are near it but once you move, it cuts out or drops the signal all together. The reason for this is because our bodies are made up of energy which is just another frequency. The frequency at which you operate can either heal or destroy a person. It's up to

ALL YOUR MOSAIC SELF

80

you to decide which frequency you want to operate at. What type of station would you like to broadcast?

Personally, I love R&B and Soca music. I know they don't exactly go together, but they are what fuel my mornings with the good vibes I need to start my day. Ninety-nine percent of the time, these types of music are singing about love and happiness.

Here we are again with that word: happy. Remember, happiness is individually defined either through love, sex or money. You get to decide which frequency to broadcast. The point is to play the type of vibe you like. There is no way I would allow heavy metal music to stream on my radio station because it would give me a headache.

Knowing what your triggers are will not only protect you but will project you. You always want to be operating in your greatest power, so you are always moving forward, and life goals are being met. This means you have to be intentional with the things you attract, as well as the things you allow to flow through you.

If I know that a certain genre of music (or group of persons) would put me in a low vibrational state of being, then I owe it to myself to not indulge in that (or those) which do not serve my greatest good. Since I am already in tune with my personal desires and goals, I only want nice, happy tunes broadcasting from my personal radio station. One may not always be able to control what we attract (i.e., bad vibes), but we can certainly control what
we entertain.

Just like a radio requires power to operate (whether it be batteries or electricity), you must empower yourself with whatever energy you need to function at your greatest.

## Mosaic Mindset Moment

(Grab your journal or notebook)

- Can you name three things that make you smile, bring you pleasure or fill your heart with joy?

- Now are you indulging in, participating in, or reflecting on these daily, weekly or monthly?

If you answered Yes, then congratulations on effectively powering your soul/radio with good things. But if you answered No, let's find out why. I want you to ask yourself why you have not been partaking in the things that make you happy.

- When you do this, take a deep breath then close your eyes. Then write down one reason why you have not regularly been partaking in the things that make you happy:

This question could stir up some uncomfortable truths that you may have been suppressing for a long time. The purpose of this exercise is not to make you stir up past trauma, but rather expose those obstacles so we can begin to move you out of your own seemingly safe, inside, soul-dwelling museum.

It's ok if you have more than one reason that rises to the surface. But I want you to focus on one scenario at a time so that you don't overwhelm your subconscious.

If you are up to it, you can grab a separate sheet of paper and begin to list all the reasons. You can always come back to this exercise and sort through each of your now self-identified dilemmas or excuses at a later time.

- Next, with the answer given above, I want you to challenge this thought by coming up with two solutions to remove that obstacle:

You did great!

Remember to breathe. Taking deep breaths not only calms you down but it also releases the tension in your body. Yet again allowing you the opportunity to fine tune that frequency you broadcast to the world. What good would being outside in the fresh air be if you neglected to take in the healing properties of the great outdoors? If you aren't feeling your chest slowly rise then descend with each exhale, then you still have some pinned up energy that has to
be addressed.

Get out of your head! Acknowledging your awesomeness and doing the things that bring you pleasure does not mean that you are being arrogant. It means that you have tapped into the inner you and clearly identified what fuels your spirit. Indulging in those activities that are pleasurable to you is a form of self-care.

By now, we are all aware of how vital self-care is. I'd like to thank over a year in quarantine with small children for acquiring that superpower!

Sometimes self-care is viewed as selfish but it's actually the opposite. It is a manifestation of the physical energy your soul needs to broadcast at its most positive frequency. It also could be your subconscious mind's way of keeping you out of jail for losing your mind, but I digress. If more individuals would partake in self-care, the world would be brighter with all of our colorful mosaic statues just shimmering in the sunlight. We mustn't be afraid of all of our broken bits, for they are the essence of who we are.

Glitter, for example, is nothing more than thousands of cut or torn pieces of shimmery plastic. Can it be hard to work with? Yes. Will it make a huge mess if not handled properly? Absolutely. But is it not the go-to craft supply for celebrations, enhancements or highlights? Damn, Skippy! Do you think that glitter gives a damn about your feelings when it decides to explode all over you when you were just needing a tiny bit for a project? No, it does not care. It is up to you to decide whether you would like to tackle a task like glitter or simply avoid it all together because it is too much.

This takes me back to you being aware of what you attract versus what you entertain. There are some individuals that hate glitter. But I, for instance, love it! On any given day of the week, I may have on some form of glitter, be it a shirt, body lotion, makeup or shoes.

What does that mean for the persons who may come in contact with me that day? Well, that means that although you may not like it, you may have a little glitter residue after being in my presence. So, while someone may not want to entertain the idea of wearing glitter, because glitter is so easily transferred, it is their job to remove or repel what attached to them that they did not want.

That leads us to setting boundaries to protect your energy. If your mosaic statue doesn't have security and protective protocols, then it is subject to anything anybody wants to do to it. You are too valuable for that. Not everyone can afford access to your museum/garden, and that is ok. If everyone were allowed to test drive certain luxury vehicles, it would cheapen its market value and possibly degrade its social status.

Because I want to see you outside, shining, breathing and broadcasting at your highest potential, let's do another exercise to identify, establish and enforce your boundaries.

Before we can set some boundaries, we must first acknowledge our goals. Name two personal goals that you are actively pursuing right now:

(For example: I am working on my master's degree.)

What are a few things that you do or allow that take your focus off that goal?

(For example: I party with my friends too much on the weekends when I should be studying.)

Lastly, what could I do differently that would help me reach that goal without further stress or anxiety?

(For example: I could communicate to my friends that I am not available to party weekly, but that I can tolerate two parties a month without feeling overworked and unhappy.)

The sole purpose of boundaries is to protect what you have built or are building so the world can view the very best version of you. That also goes for your wellbeing. It takes great strength to not only identify your boundaries, but to enforce them. That is a vital step to oneself development and defining your worth. Honoring your boundaries is a bold representation of a person who knows their own worth, which is the epitome of selfcare.

How can you effectively walk in your purpose if you don't even believe you are worthy of all the things God has promised you? The answer is you can't. I'm not a fan of the word impossible but to skip this boundary enforcement opportunity damn near makes it impossible to level up.

Recall those luxury vehicles we talked about. Focusing on cost, rather than access and availability this time. It is easy to see how one could feel that their prices (often being tens of thousands of dollars more than the average car) can inflict sticker shock or distain from those who cannot afford it. But Rolls Royce does not care. They are not in the business of making their vehicles affordable for all to drive. Rolls Royce understand the quality they put into their vehicles is a reflection of the price, and that not everyone is going to be able to afford it. This is also why it is so important to design what you want your life to look like. A person can never win an argument with someone who is standing in their truth and planted in their personally cultivated mosaic garden.

Every day we have the autonomy to decide what type of energies we will absorb, multiply or deny. This includes what you are watching on TV, and what you view on social media or see outside.

Earlier we wrote down some triggers. How do think continuously entertaining those things that are not adding to your sense of self-worth is helping you shine to your highest potential? The reality is, they aren't. Those things are simply distractions. It's up to you to eliminate as many distractions as possible along your discovery path to self-worth, so that you cannot help but turn the focus on you.

I know you are probably reading this like, "Girl, I am not trying to be the center of attention everywhere I go." To which my response is, "Get used to it, babes!" You are crafting this beautiful mosaic structure that is too great to keep contained. I know it
is uncomfortable at times, but I promise you will get used to being uncomfortable.

Walking into a space and changing the atmosphere will become a normal part of life for you because you understand that your high positive frequency is essential to transforming those lower vibrational situations, or individuals, for that matter.

This isn't an act of being conceited either. As long as you are moving with integrity in your awesomeness, then you will never be conceited, for we have learned that to operate from a place of self-worth is both a duty and pleasure. You are most valuable to people when showing the best version of you that you have to offer. That type of energy is infectious.

I want you to challenge yourself after reading this chapter. The next time you have an event or meeting to attend, I want you to confidently show up and lock eyes with three people in the room.

Now, before we just go connecting with any folk, remember our boundaries and specific demographics that we are allowing access to our shiny souls. This is not a free for all; although some may residually catch the shine, that isn't our focus. We are broadcasting a sort of invitation vibe to allow those on our same frequency to enter our garden/presence while empowering them to stand outside their museum as well.

You may find that this experience may evoke better conversations, connections or even opportunities, which is exactly what we are going for. The best version of ourselves is often afraid to be outside because there are far more negative thoughts floating around our brains than positive ones, and we may not have enough tools to challenge those thoughts.

But what you are building by connecting with those three people in that moment is evidence. Evidence that you will not die if you lock eyes with a stranger. You are also establishing the fact you know who you are and what you came to offer to the world. Operating in such a manner gives our spirits the room they need to grow and glow as brightly as possible.

Try this experiment and document your feelings here. Come back to it often to see how far you have grown:

- Today, I locked eyes with a stranger and emotionally I felt:

- What physical response did your body experience?

- What was the response of the other person?

- Lastly, what could you do differently next time?

Do you feel all that power flowing through you at this moment? Baby, you have arrived outside! The great outdoors. Don't put your statue back as punishment, regressing back to your old ways. Your true self is too great to be confined by hypothetical walls made up of the ideals of individuals who have yet to acknowledge their own self-worth. Be greater because it is who you are. Simply existing in your own divinity is precisely the permission others around you need to feel empowered to go out and seek their own. So, continue to lock eyes, smile and shine, because you are so divine!

# Counseling
# A Courting Crown

## Alyse Janel

I f every heartbroken woman could relive their love story, I believe many would, and then educate their admiring children on how to avoid their heartaches while they explore the dating world.

Many modern women would reconsider the time they wasted dating men where it led to them feeling drained, incomplete, undervalued, and with lower self-esteem. I'm also sure there are plenty of men that feel the same way; so this doesn't solely disregard that men haven't been heart-broken as well.

However, it actually leads us to wonder what changed from courting for marriage, generations ago, and dating now. It seemed as if it was easier for our grandparents to find their soulmate with fewer resources compared to us having access to the entire world at our fingertip. If we could see into the future and see how our temporary love interest would end; we'll be a lot more open to being coached and counseled by those who survived relationship hardships, wouldn't you agree?

Truth be told, we have these figures in our lives to protect us and guide us through love interest, and they're called fathers. Most cultures where the men are the patriarchy, pride themselves on ensuring their family is protected, provided for, and their children grow on to then past the torch and create their own successful families.

Unfortunately, due to known traumas in urban America; we lack responsible strong father figures and by far this will not be an attack on those men. We will briefly take a moment to understand that minority men struggle in their own rights and have been attacked from every direction from government sabotage, war on drugs, and even the feminist movement. So every girl hasn't had the privilege of enjoying their true love but experienced the trauma of abandonment, disappointment, and left some beautiful women feeling Pretty Broken.

So, we as women must take the oath to ourselves that we will heal, be accountable, receive the proper counseling, and give ourselves a chance to be properly loved. And it all begins with us and accepting and loving ourselves first. Like all the queens we've learned in history; we must prep ourselves to be fit for the crown.

We must care for our inner self as well as our exterior. Mental wellness must be a priority, and this doesn't just stem from just a few good self-help books, but applying the advice we receive, even if the truth hurts. Understanding that self-awareness is a difficult task and will lead to some dark dungeons we've been avoiding for some time. Taking accountability for any failures due to our own pride and ignorance.

It's alright to acknowledge that one doesn't know, or guidance is needed even at this stage of life. Sometimes it's absolutely necessary to approach an old scenario with a new mindset or guidance from an unbiased perspective. This doesn't mean that it's the end of the world as we know it because we were wrong. We just need to slightly humble ourselves and state that the way we thought we were winning, isn't clearly working for us.

We must be more observant of the signs in front of us. No more will we be blindsided by the red flags, justify poor behavior, or being the emotional punching bag. It's more damaging holding on than letting go and waiting for someone who's not showing true interest to change. Isolation might temporarily be needed until we've unmasked our demons and proceed in acknowledging our past rather than not being triggered by it. We cannot continue to tell ourselves lies in order to live in this make-belief life we told ourselves.

Another entity we must focus our attention to is our physical health and image. Most queens we've admired were beautiful and yes, in shape. They take pride in ensuring that they are attractive, and they can turn the heads of many. We're not stating that all queens are a cookie cutter image, but they are for sure beautiful inside and out. They are indeed unique and have an alluring aura about themselves.

You cannot attempt to attract all good things when you're feeling crummy on the inside. We must be completely mindful of the things we allow to enter our body and soul. It's so easy to get caught up in the rush of life that we neglect ourselves. However, the information I share with you is not brand new nor will it be the only time you here this advice. You must stay hydrated beautiful, drink plenty of water.

Most of the time you'll see many underlining issues stem from

dehydration along with poor eating habits. You must take pride in your body and your attire. When you step outside you don't only represent yourself, but your family, your (future) partner, and
the culture.

We must also hold each other accountable, and not gang up on one another, when hardcore facts are presented. Great example, when the Queen of Comedy Monique, herself stated, that we must take pride when we go out in public black queens, and that mean taking the hair bonnets and pajamas off when out in public where other ethnicities can use that representation to define us as a whole.

Rather than acknowledging that she was providing genuine wisdom from a woman that travels the world; she was dragged across social media and criticized for her comments.

Any woman that's willing to continue to grow and improve would have easily agreed with her and supported and guided another young lady in their life too with the same advice. You don't just represent yourself when you're in public, but you represent every black woman those other cultures criticize and judge. The world is always watching, so be sure to give them something good to look at!

In order to receive all the benefits that you seek from a king, you must recognize that success leaves clues, and many wise queens and kings have left these clues. They can be found in the Bible, in ancient teachings, through therapy, meditation, and other sources such as our favorite controversial podcast hosts, we love to hate, but we know deep down they're telling the truth. Now if you choose to ignore the clues because they humble your pride or make you feel vulnerable then you can't compare yourself to the women who's willing to hold themselves accountable and make the change. Many black women have come to terms that they no longer want to follow in the footsteps of generational curses. We're starting to see that the way we've been moving throughout life in survival mode no longer serves us when finding love.

We're loosening the strongholds that society has labeled us with as being non-supportive, angry, bitter, independent strong women. We see our worth and nothing is wrong with being independent and strong until it takes on a masculine energy that most men aren't willing to deal with on a long-term basis.

We must accept that the strong exterior is due to our soft feelings being fractured. So, we must heal and be willing to move in peace, harmony, and submission. Again, this doesn't demeanor you nor does it disqualify you, but you must make the adjustment and be willing to change to receive something new and never experienced before. Marriage and partnership is a matter of constant compromise, respect, teachable moments, and a ton of selfless acts.

The word submission nowadays is equivalent to a curse word or worst, slavery nowadays. Only in our culture has taken care of a man's needs looked upon as a choir or a punishment, but we want the red carpet rolled out for us. Submission isn't about shutting up and taking order, but its more about cooperation, trusting the direction, and being a team player.

Although, I might get some backlash from our modern-day women; the old way was the right way and the outcome would be, you can still get everything you desire today from your man if you play your part. Why, because it' s in each of our nature to fulfill naturally. Most men if asked, don't mind paying for a lifestyle if they're respected and treated nicely. I also know women who support and submit to their man who not only have a care-free life but they still get to be BOSS in their own lane.

However, entitlement and audacity have run completely rampant in our community, and we must restore it. We're losing our uniqueness by being copycats and admiring those that get a paycheck to flaunt all their business on the worldwide net. Remember us women control who we have sex with but men ultimately control who gets married. Ask yourself truthfully what man wants to wife something that can be purchased to the highest bidder.

For centuries, kings have sought out conservative, respectable, natural feminine women. There's absolutely no issue in knowing your worth women but we must be respectful to all, including the men we desire. So, you must be more than a beautiful body, especially in today's time where everyone has access to several options at the sight of an app. Looks alone will not get the job done, but it does help.

We know our worth and the men we desire know theirs too, and not willing to deal with the healed version of ourselves. So, you must be mindful of the way you portray ourselves. If you truly desire a man that makes you feel special the same thing should be reciprocated, through self-love and dignity too. Showcase that being with you is an amazing deal that no one would want to miss out, whether that's a friend or a partner in life. You are not for sale.

Truth is there's nothing wrong with wanting to live in the traditional gender role where the men take care of a majority of all financial responsibilities while protecting you and the household. However, you must be willing to walk in the role of the woman with the desire to be chosen as a wife. You must wholeheartedly consider your man when you choose to be his partner.

Please note, these are husband benefits or someone who at least made a commitment to you; boyfriends are disposable but hopefully they are auditioning for a permanent position in your life. P.S, it doesn't take years to know if someone is the one, and ladies please don't sabotage the opportunity if he wants to lead and give you a title. You have a lifetime to get to know each other, catch him while he's head over hills for you, and you two can spend a lifetime getting to know each other.

We are more than deserving of the crown we demand others to recognize without coercion and manipulation. We won't just call ourselves queens, because it's a trendy cute greeting, but we will walk with dignity that others won't be able to overlook; standing out from the crowd so we will attract those who admire, inspire, and committed to courting for our crown.

# Purposeful Alignment

## Talia Elise

Hey, Sis!

I know you have read the other chapters, and now it's my time to assist you with alignment! How does one get in alignment, you say? I'm glad you asked! Now that I have your attention, let's start with this:

Alignment *(definition):* brought into line or proper arrangement.

Purpose *(definition):* the reason for which something is done or created or for which something exists.

How does one come into alignment?

**- Heart posture of gratitude:** No matter what is going on in your life—good or bad—you should trust God completely. If you're not grateful for the things He is doing now, how can you be grateful for the things He will do?

- **Pray:** Prioritize your time with God. Intimate time with God is important for alignment. (Draw near to God, and He will draw near to you.)

- **Declutter:** Sis, your space is important; it will set the tone for how you feel, physically and mentally.

- **Time management:** Be a good steward over your time. Watch who and what you give yourself too. Time wasted is time you can't get back!

- **Be intentional:** Stay focused, prepare and be ready for it.

Now, once you have done these things (and its doesn't have to be in the order I gave), be still and listen!

Purpose is not a destination, but a journey. Don't think that once you find your purpose, you have arrived. Your purpose is forever in motion and forever evolving. Each level of your purpose will require a different version of you.

Let me ask you something...who are you? And who has God called you to be? But when I ask this question, I'm asking outside of being a mother, wife, sister, daughter, etc. Who are you? What has God called you to do? Purpose beings when these questions can be answered in confidence.

When someone says, "Talia who are you?" Baby, before I didn't know. Now, I got a whole list for them. Who is Talia, you asked? I am a daughter of the king, a world changer, influencer, prayer warrior, generational breaker, mountain mover, author, speaker and millionaire in the making! And I say all of that with my chest, but that was not always the case.

Once, I was broken and in search of the women I am today and I'm still learning and evolving into myself. Life has a way of breaking you; things arise that make you question if God even loves you. But my advice to you, is *don't quit*! Push through it. There is greatness in the process.

Let me tell you, in finding my purpose, I had to cry, kick and scream, and all in that order. But there is beauty in the pain. As Fabolous says, "Don't be bitter, be better."

Sometimes we are told that this generation is defined by the world. But that is not true,

Because God says that before He formed it, He knew you and me, and that speaks volumes.

But what if you're not spiritual and God is not really your thing?

*Purpose* is the reason for which something is done or created, or for which something exists. You can always find your purpose; you just have to be still and listen. I know you have heard something like "Obedience is our responsibility, and the outcome is God's." Let me give you an example of what I mean.

I got married young and never thought that I would be divorced. But the crazy thing is that I didn't find my purpose and identity until it ended. Sometimes the biggest struggles in life will turn out to be some of our biggest blessings, if we just hold on.

As women, we wear so many hats that our own identity and purpose often get loss. Don't get me wrong, there are probably plenty of women who are thriving in purpose, married and all. I'm just saying that my journey was different.

We can have these great plans for our lives and then God hits you with the redirect. But you know what? I understand now that the redirect was necessary because God was protecting me from things that I didn't see at the time.

For years I blamed myself for ignoring who I was and putting so much focus on others' happiness instead of my own. I compromised a lot and it cost me time that I can't get back.

Sis, if your married, divorced, single and/or in a complicated situation, don't lose yourself! Be in a consistent posture of learning and evolving into your better self.

I pray that I continue to see myself the way God does and to have the courage to go after that version of myself. Fear is one heck of distraction and, yes, I say *distraction* because no matter how much fear tries to show up, you have to rise up and face it. A purpose will find you and be fulfilled in the earth.

I often hear people say, "If I could tell the younger me what I know now, I would have avoided so much stress and heartache."

If you're anything like me, I was one of God's hardheaded daughters! God would send a word through a person, song, or dream, and I would do the opposite and suffer the consequences. But I learned in my journey that your stubbornness or choosing not to listen doesn't stop your purpose. It does put a delay on it, and that, Sis, is not even worth the setback.

Accountability is the first thing. Not pointing fingers in a situation but taking responsibility for what you have done. Because sometimes the delay be your fault, Sis! Swallow that pills and
move forward.

That *something*, that purpose, requires self-reflection and this is important when you are seeking a purpose, because you're not perfect and you can't just walk into one like it's meant for you. Self-reflection allows you to humble yourself and correct your heart posture. Your purpose is always bigger than you, and the mission is always for God to get the glory! So self-reflecting allows you to do that and for God to mold and shape you.

Here is my testimony on finding myself and discovering purpose. I got married young and although I thought it would be forever, it ended. That was when I came into my full purpose, and the worsts things in my life ended up being the best blessings of my life. Could I say that while I was going through it? Heck, no! But the woman I am now is allowing me to say that.

Here is what I learned: There is beauty in letting go and being redirected. My divorce birthed something on the inside of me that was hard to explain in the beginning. But, oh, when it manifested it was a sight to see.

Purpose requires you to do the work and be obedient through the process, even when it doesn't feel good. I learned that it was okay to feel what you're going through and that you don't have to mask it. Why? Because the mind is the enemy's playground. He can't attack or use what you don't reveal, and it's the "I'm okays" and "I'm goods" through which he tries to play you mentally.

So, what I had to do was tell God I was angry, unhappy, confused, anxious, depressed and that I wouldn't make it if he didn't step in. So, when my life started to unfold in front of people, as embarrassed as I was, I learned to say, "I'm not okay, but in time, I will be." And, Sis, that was the game changer for me. I realized that I accepted what had happened and was in the next step of learning to let it go.

My process was long, and I ain't going to lie and say it was a beautiful one, because ya girl went through it. I cried and questioned myself a lot, as well as what God wanted from me. I thought my purpose had been fulfilled when I became a mom and had two little people counting on me, but God had called me for something greater.

You know the crazy part about purpose? Sometimes you don't feel you're the woman for the job and you question or try to rearrange it to make it fit what you thought it should be. And sometimes God be like, "Girl, if you don't stop..." (Well, that's what I know God be saying to me! Don't judge me.)

I honestly didn't feel like I was enough, or I was embarrassed by my testimony. But as I grew, I learned that there was power in my voice and in speaking my truth. That even if I wasn't for everybody, I was called to somebody. That the me being the blueprint to someone's healing was for God to get the glory. That sometimes just taking the steps and walking in obedience can also be a breakthrough for yourself.

We live in a time where social media is our outlet, and I'm not saying don't use it, but what I am saying is to be discerning. Sometimes our feelings can take us down emotional rollercoasters if we don't understand how to control them.

Trust me, I was the queen of *knuck if you buck* and responded to what I felt in the moment. I allowed my emotions to take me to places that I now regret, and I wish had responded better. The beautiful thing about growth and purpose is that your mindset changes. Now you won't find me acting out of character. I am the queen of unbothered and peace is now my potion! (Let the church say amen.)

Also, don't let people, social media or anything else rush your process. However, I will also say, don't stay in one place forever. Remember, a small step is still progress. Celebrate the milestones of your growth and don't compare your progress to others. Instead, use it as fuel to keep going. If God, did it for them, He most certainly will do it for you.

Even with purpose, you have to understand and trust timing. The Bible declares, "To everything there is a season, and a time to every purpose under the heaven." (*Ecclesiastes 3:1.*) One, you don't need to be in a rush, and two, don't procrastinate.

Always remember that there is room for everyone in the kingdom. Just because someone might be doing something similar doesn't mean God can't call you too. If you're called to it, then it can be fulfilled in the earth.

Comparison is the thief of joy, so focus and stand on what you are called to. Remember that when we focus on our assignment and position ourselves correctly, God will enlarge our territory. So, what I'm saying is, be a good steward over what God has given you and he will multiply the rest!

When you are going through the process, you don't understand timing and seasons. You just want your feelings to get under control, as you feel like you're being pulled in multiple directions. This why you have to be still and listen, because God always sends a word.

But my question to you is, *are you listening?* If you're not, it's because what you see is not what you thought it would be. So, you get stuck with trying to fix or control things and not remembering what your purpose is.

I know my chapter is church, but, hey, it's my foundation and I wouldn't be the diamond writer that I am if I don't give honor where honor is due. I owe God everything and I will never apologize for it. I'm not for everybody, but I'm for somebody. My purpose is to change lives and help other dope women get there too.

Now this brings me to this question, *who is your tribe?* Who assisting and lifting you up on your way to your destiny? Who you connect yourself with is so important because without God— and the amazing group of women in my corner—I wholeheartedly don't know where I would be at all in my life.

Listen, I could go on and on and on about the women who God has placed in my life. Shout out to them! Why? Because there ain't no hood like my sisterhood! They have prayed, fasted, uplifted and gone to war in the spirit for me. In the moments where I wanted to drift away and hide under a rock, they wouldn't let me. They filled my cup when I had nothing left and that, Sis, is what sisterhood is all about.

So, remember, when God gives you divine friendship and they bring you closer to who you are, keep them and cherish it. My tribe does this when anyone is going through a tough time, and they don't want to talk. We give them space but then we are like, "Yeaaah, time's up! You've been here too long, it's time to fight and push to the next level."

Sometimes you've also got to know that not every friendship fits with your purpose, and that is okay. It doesn't mean that you love them any less, it just means that life has put you on different paths.

Healthy friendships are my heart's desire. Really, just healthy relationships, period! My heart has been through the worst, even though I am whole and healing. I got to prescreen! First question, "Who sent you?" Because the enemy will send you a distraction in the form of friendships or relationships.

You must be able to discern and know how to remove yourself gracefully. You won't know that a distraction is a distraction until its done distracting you. *Whew, chile, that was a mouthful!* But it was food for thought. How many of us have been distracted and are like, "What in the world?!" That's why, even when you are in pursuit of something, you must be diligent in occupying your time. Because time doesn't wait for anyone. Luckily, God can restore time and get you back on track.

For me, when pursuing my purpose, the enemy distracted me with counterfeits. I had decided to fully pursue my purpose and focus on me, and here come Mr. Fine! Sometime loneliness will have you operating in a place where purpose can't find you. What I mean by that is that no good thing that God sends should distract you or not be a help in you pursing purpose.

My prayer is that when the distraction comes, I will see the enemy's plan and move accordingly.

Sis, I can't begin to tell you how greatly this discussion has blessed me. Purpose is not an easy road, but it's a road worth the travel. To be who you were destined to be is one dope achievement. Not only is my greatest accomplishment—being the mom of two amazing children—but it's also seeing God do just what he said and more. I have this unspeakable joy and the world can't take that from me. I know that my pain has served a purpose and that my voice will heal broken people.

No matter what you see in the natural world and even when you feel like God has forgotten, I want you to remember that the Lord will withhold no good thing from you. He knows the plans He has for you and that it will all work out for the best.

Even if you find yourself in a place where you feel purpose has left, speak life into and rise!

The Bible declares, "As a man thinks, so is he," so here are some affirmations to speak into your life:

- I will fulfill my purpose on the earth.

- I am fearfully and wonderfully made.

- There is room for me in the kingdom.

- No good thing will the lord withhold from me.

- I believe and will trust in my process.

# Help Her
# With Her Crown

## Skyler Freeman

S is, I know it's easy to want to challenge her, and, honestly, look down on her, but have you ever considered what it took for her to get to where she is today?

Through heartache and pain, she is not exempt from life's troubles and tribulations. Everyone that looks perfect in the eyes of another may very well be broken on the inside. For instance, I have been judged and bullied by other women all because one woman assumed I was better than her.

When the reality is, I actually would have loved to be friends, build a connection or even partner together in leaving a legacy! But with society today, it is easy to knock her crown down and step on it rather than helping her keep it straight.

With a society of women made to tear each other apart, we, as women, collectively have to look at history. Our history shows us we envy each other, break one another and assault each other

with
no remorse.

Michele Obama has a beautiful quote that says, "The difference between a broken community and a thriving one is the presence of women who are valued."

I truly believe in that motto. When I look at the different cultures and places around the world, I can see the way in which women are either valued or devalued, and the ending result is the value of those around those same women.

Women are made to bring love and support to humanity, collectively, but how can one truly thrive when she has so many other species that are just like her, grabbing at her crown and trying to tear it down?

But let's break this down on a deeper level. This may ruffle some feathers but I'm saying this out of pure love, and I hope you receive it this way.

The base of our problem is that the tearing down of each other starts at home. What are you doing every day to impact, uplift or help another woman? Are you positive? Do you even smile when you see another sis walking in your direction? These are the things that will shift the culture, uplift and change the way we, as women, operate on a daily basis.

I know it's so hard to swallow that pill of seeing her driving the car you dream of, or, better yet, wearing the outfit that you don't even work out enough to fit in, but seriously, c'mon, we can truly be better and can do more together than apart.

Another woman wearing her crown does not mean you are less than her. Actually, you and her together wearing a crown is a powerful duo. I like to think of women as a special society.

Listen, we give birth to nations. You can't tell me if we all get on one accord we can't shift and change the world. It's up to all of us to focus on one mission and agree to shift the culture. Having a supportive community of women uplifting and refusing to tear down one another is what owning a crown is about.

I remember vividly being in my despair and misery and yet refusing to hate another woman because, at the end of the day, I had to understand that the woman's thinking could have been a taught behavior. Half of the time that is the case; most women don't choose to be hateful, bitter, mean and nasty, but a lot of women learn this behavior indirectly. Maybe her mom was bitter and a mean woman and as a little girl she mimicked this behavior. So many women in our society don't even understand that they have a mental negative personality based on unprecedented circumstances.

As triggering as it is, this is a hard truth. I only ever speak from experience. I was indirectly influenced by negativity but because God had a calling on me as a little girl, I knew it was not healthy nor beneficial for me. I was the black butterfly of the family, always questioning the indirectly taught behaviors, and for it I would get slapped in the face or beat, but I knew this was not the right way
to be.

I say all of this to show that some young girls grow up thinking that this behavior is normal or healthy and turn into grown women with this same mindset. I cry for them because hate is a learned and taught behavior. We don't grow up hating people for what they have or how they look. We mimic the environment we have been accustomed to.

So, my question to you is: have you been indirectly influenced by negativity in your life? And if so, have you indirectly impacted another woman's life negatively? Did you help her with her crown or knock it down?

But ultimately, Sis, do you wear your own crown? Wearing a crown is not about being better or having more. You see, it's actually about companionship, leadership, understanding and acknowledging. It starts with the self.

Self-acceptance and loving you for you. That way you don't have the time or room to hate. Help another woman with her crown; you never know, it may very well be the way to your own breakthrough and liberation.

# Her Voice

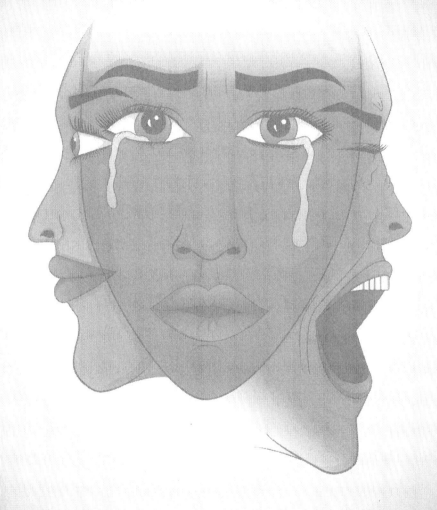

# Can You
# Hear Me Now?

## Jessica Newman

The beeping sound is getting louder in my ear. Everyone is just standing around with a confused look on their faces.

Somebody? Anybody? Do something! Why are we just standing here waiting? Why aren't we doing all that we can do? What are we going to do?

I'm so lost in my thoughts right now that I don't even realize the beeping has stopped. Flatline.

In this moment right here, I no longer exist. In this moment right here, my representative has come on the scene. Allow me to introduce myself. Hello, my name is Unseen, Overlooked and Unheard.

I thought the best thing for me to do at that very second was to run out the room and try to find a way out of hell. All I kept saying to myself was, "I don't know what we are going to do."

This was the first time I had ever seen my father cry. He had this worried look on his face and was just as lost and confused as I was.

Dear God, what have you done? I mean, really, God, what were you thinking when you did this?

I turned back around and faced her room. She was lying there, lifeless. And everyone continued to just stand there.

My heart was empty. I was hurt and confused. My life was over I would never know real love again.

There are no self-help books or counseling sessions or group meetings to prepare you for the death of your mother. It's just something that people tell you you'll get through. That you will eventually learn to live with it. Although that is a load of crap.

Twenty-three years later, and I'm still not who I was before she was snatched from my life. Yes, snatched. I say snatched because I didn't have a choice in the matter.

I remember every night after I was told my mom was sick, I asked God to make her better. I asked him not to take her away. But clearly, he had other plans.

No one ever asked me my opinion or how I felt about how they were handling my mother's care. All they would say is, "You're young, don't worry about it." Well, how in the hell am I not
going to worry about my mother? I was confused then, and I'm still
confused now.

I was filled with so much rage and anger, but no one knew it. I kept it all to myself. Immediately, my representative stepped on the scene. She was quiet, she was strong, she could overcome anything. She never spoke up. Always did her best to please everyone. Goodness, this chick was a mess! It was crazy how well I played the game. Or so I thought.

When people used to ask me, "How are you feeling? Do you need anything?" I would always say, "I'm good." But I was mentally f**ked up. I just wanted my mother back. Crazy to think that I thought I could bargain with God for her to come back.

I don't even think my family really knew how messed up I was. I mean, they were all grown with their own lives. I guess they figured I would grow out of it and move on eventually.

Negative.

My representative was a force to be reckoned with, doing any and everything to fill a void that could never be filled. There she goes again, screwing that dude. There she goes again, drinking that booze. There she goes again, just sin, sin, sin. Damn, someone come and get her. She is about to self-destruct.

And that's what I did, until one day my representative met someone who was way more f**ked up than she was.

If no one heard my cries during my mother's sickness and death, they did not hear them during my tumultuous relationship that I began at the age of 19.

When I met Smoke, I was damaged goods. I did not really know myself or even love myself. I was just looking for someone to love me. Hell, I would even have settled for a strong like.

Smoke stepped on the scene like Captain Save-a-Hoe. He was all that and a bag of chips plus a 25-cent blow pop. I couldn't believe back then that someone as fine and smooth as he was, would like me.

But I soon found out Smoke was full of smoke. Many of us know the signs of physical abuse, but emotional and mental abuse that can get a little tricky.

Smoke played the game well. He made me believe I was all he needed and wanted. I ignored all the warning signs and just focused on how good he looked. I really couldn't believe he wanted me; I was starstruck. Funny thing is, how can you be starstruck by someone who is just a regular around the way guy?

There were so many moments in our relationship where I wasn't heard. I had questions about so many things Smoke was doing, but I was too afraid to ask and hear an answer that would mess up my perfect fantasy. It came to a point where I could no longer hide my feelings, and I had to find out what was really going on.

The hard questions had to come out, and one day I had the opportunity to do so. "Who is she? Is it your baby? Do you love her? What is she to you?"

Of course, all these questions were followed by lies and half-truths. But the loyal woman that I was pretended to believe him. Deep down inside, I knew I was a fool, but remember, I was blinded by his outside beauty. He stood in front of me trying to talk his way out of it, but I sunk so deep into my thoughts that I barely remembered anything he said. I was lost. At that moment, he had won my soul, and I gave up.

Days, months, and years passed, and those same old questions continued to repeat themselves over the course of our relationship. At some point I just stopped asking. I did my own investigations, took the information and laughed it off. Yes, I laughed. Smoke was never going to be honest and admit his wrongdoings. He was just going to fill my head with lies and hopes and dreams that he would be a
better man.

Laughter was good for me. It made me feel like I had some control. I kept thinking to myself if I just keep laughing it off, maybe I would wake up and it would just be a bad joke someone was playing on me.

But just like my family, Smoke didn't hear my cries. I begged him time and time again to just love me. I asked him what I could do to help him to change, but his response was always the same: "It's not you, it's me." Laughter is good for the soul, I heard, but, in this case, laughter just proved how mentally disturbed I really was.

What's crazy is Smoke would join in on the laughter with me. I guess he thought laughter was going to save us, but all it did was continue to allow our relationship to die right in front of our eyes.

FLATLINE.

For years I was confused, lost, hurt, angry and empty inside. The same feelings I had when losing my mother were back again. I thought God sent Smoke to save me, to relieve me from my pain and past trauma. Once again, I cried out to God, "Why is this happening to me?" But instead of saying, "Bring her back," I was asking God to take him away. Let's just say God did not answer my prayers the way I wanted him to.

What God did for me was he gave me the opportunity to finally listen to myself. I had to deal with the real issues of why I felt like no one ever heard my cries. I had to find out who I really was and get rid of my representative. I had to finally heal and listen to God, instead of asking him to just listen to me. I knew God was hearing me, but I just never took the time to listen to what he had to say.

I loved Smoke and even though he had some messed-up ways about himself, I truly believed he loved me. He loved our children, he was a hard worker, supported me in everything I wanted to do, and he tried to be a good husband while fighting his own demons.

To be honest, he was a better friend then husband. I could talk to him about anything except for his lack of respect for our union. But even with all the counseling, late night talks and just trying to figure things out between us, I still was lost and did not know the real me.

I remember the day I found myself. What's funny is I wasn't even trying to find myself. I was at church, getting ready to serve in the children's nursery, and before service started, our group leader asked if anyone had any prayer requests. Usually when this question was asked, I quietly bowed my head and didn't make any direct eye contact. However, this day was different. Something came over me that I couldn't understand or describe. I felt warm all over and goosebumps ran up and down my arm. Before I could even swallow my words and look away, my hand went up and I shouted, "I have a prayer request."

I told everyone that my marriage was in trouble and said that I needed help. I didn't give many details since I was in a room full of people who I didn't want to judge me. The group leader prayed for God's will to be done in my marriage.

After everyone left, I walked quietly to my room, not really knowing if my prayers were going to be answered. But I was surely glad I let some of my secrets out and thought that maybe this time God could help me.

A few minutes after, when I was in the nursery, the group leader came in and asked if we could speak privately. I nodded hesitantly but went willingly. He asked if we could talk more about what was going on in my marriage.

The worlds left my tongue so fast. It was such a relief to finally be able to tell someone all my dirty little secrets about my not so perfect marriage. I talked about all the cheating, the other children, the lies, the manipulation, the hurt, the fear. I said it all.

He listened quietly and I just knew he was probably thinking, this lady is really messed up, there is no hope. But he continued to nod and listen intensely. When I finally finished, he asked me, "What do you want? Do you want to stay, or do you want to leave?"

In the past, if someone had asked this same question, I had always said, "Of course I want to stay." But this time, I wasn't sure. I didn't know if I had any fight left in me. I did not know if Smoke was ever going to hear me or see the real me and love me the way I needed to be loved.

I sat quietly and pondered what would life be like if I threw in the towel. So many thoughts ran through my mind. I just wasn't sure. I knew I wanted different, something more than the fake laugher and corruptive love. Would I ever find the love that I was looking for? The love I had longed for ever since my mother died. I wasn't sure and I believed God wanted me to just listen to him.

So, I asked the group leader to pray for God to intervene, to help me see clearly and to guide me in the right direction. The leader prayed over me. I got up and I felt different. I felt lighter and I was ready to see how God was going to show up and show out in my life.

My life changed. No, it wasn't instantly. Days turned into months and months turned into years, but I prayed faithfully and just trusted God each day. While God was working on my marriage, I was working on myself, learning how to love me and learning my worth. This wasn't an easy task because I had to face a lot of ugly truths about myself. But I was beginning to like the "real" me. I was no longer allowing Smoke or anyone else to manipulate or walk all over me. I valued myself and set boundaries. I was no longer tolerating Smoke's foolishness and he knew it was time for him to shape up or ship out.

Smoke and I, throughout this time, had real, honest, downright ugly conversations. But these conversations helped. I finally spoke up and he finally heard me. Not only did Smoke start to listen, but I began to speak up for myself within my family. I grew up after 23 years of living a lie, holding on to the death of my mother.

I found me. It was so nice to meet her again. Happy, patient, fearless, loving me. She was everything I had hoped for, everything I prayed for. I was ready to enjoy my so-called new life.

I couldn't believe I no longer had to wonder if people could hear me, or if people were really listening to me. I said things that needed to be said and I let everyone else figure out how they wanted to deal with it. I no longer hid or second-guessed myself. I spoke my truth and was ready to deal with the consequences that came with it.

This road I have traveled has not always been easy, but it sure has been worth it. Every day I continue to pray for my marriage, for my healing and for protection from my representative. I pray I always will stand in my truth and remember to love me first. I pray that I will always be seen, always be heard, and never be overlooked again. I am looking forward to the day that all my dreams come true, and I finally never have to question if anyone can really hear me.

# Easier Said
# Than Done

## Dyisha Parker

*"We have all experienced life's unexpected moments.*
*They have the potential to change the course of our lives."*

How did I get here? I don't think anybody gets married with the intention of getting a divorce, at least, I didn't.

Let's back up. I found out I was expecting at the beginning of my second trimester and my world changed. I never wanted kids; you can ask anybody that knows me! However, who knew my daughter would be the one who actually saved me?

Living life, having fun without a care in the world, needless to say, I was shocked when I found out. I mean, I was the one who barely got in trouble and tried to live on the "straight and narrow" path.

I was fully grown, but still definitely scared to say something to my parents, especially my dad. I was so scared that I told my dad via text on my way to Bible study.

My daughter's father and I got married ten days before I was due. Talk about a lot at one time, whew!

I worked up until the day I had her, literally. I mean, I called from the hospital bed, got ready to return to work and *bam!* No job. They say finances can definitely be trouble in a marriage, and I was about to find out what that meant. Maternity leave, no job and bills still coming regardless. Did we lack anything? No, but having a family that was able to help was definitely a blessing.

After being separated for a year—including me moving to Florida during that time to see if a change in location would help—I earned another degree. While working full-time, being in school full-time and raising a toddler, my strength and patience was tested.

Naturally, we tried to work things out. We still went to family functions together, he would come visit me in Florida and I even moved back to Maryland with a different job opportunity, but in
the end, we still went our separate ways. Did I want a divorce? of course not!

Still trying to see if this would work out, the inevitable happened...I was served. I wasn't going to file for one, but he wanted it, so he filed. There was no need to contest it because nothing was going to change. It hurt like hell though, I can't lie. How ironic, the divorce was final exactly one month after our third anniversary.

Not really wanting a divorce, it was hard to accept for a long time. A good friend, a brother in Christ, told me about a book he was reading with his book club called *Codependent No More*, written by Melody Beattie.

That book was life changing! A sense of peace and calm came over me like I had never experienced before. It was like God was saying, "I have you, Daughter, don't worry about a thing." My whole perspective changed.

The question then became, "How are we going to raise this vibrant and energetic child together in peace?" It was not easy. Moving on to other relationships can be hard, especially when a child is involved. Meeting a serious significant other for the other parent can be tough. It can make you wonder, *what does he or she have, that I don't have?*

When it comes to our child(ren), I must say women will do anything to find out about a person. I had some mutual friends with the current partner of my ex. Naturally, I asked about the person who was around my child (this was prior to me even meeting her).

She was friends with a cousin of mine that was very particular about who she dealt with, so yes, I reached out to my cousin. I explained the situation and she was like, "Yeah, she is good people." That's all I wanted to know; that my child was safe in her presence. I know that sounds crazy, but I had to know for myself.

Divorce can change things, but it does not end the family. This is not always an easy task as it takes growth and maturity on both ends. It was not always easy for me when this journey began. It was pure chaos and if I'm honest, hell. The struggle is real and trying to get participation from the other parent can be tiring.

As a side note, you have to make sure you are completely over your ex, or the enemy will definitely play with your mind. I know from experience! Everything from, "See, he won't even get him or her and he is up the street with his new boo," to "He claims not to have money for school supplies from Dollar Tree, but can be over at his boo's house...he has to get gas to come over this way, doesn't he?"

Trust me when I say this: kids know more than what you think! They pick up on everything! I don't know if it comes from being in the womb and they feel our vibes, but they definitely know when something is off, spoken or not.

I felt defeated, like I failed as a parent because the family wasn't still together. But when your child pats you on the shoulder or gives that hug and says, "It's going to be okay, don't cry," motivation hits a new high!

How can you and your former spouse continue to parent your child(ren) as a cohesive unit? Well, I'm glad you asked! The first thing to do is to heal. That goes for both parties.

I found a job down south, so for me part of my healing was moving and getting into a different environment. Was it hard? Of course, because my child was no longer a few minutes away from her dad. But when you are both on the "struggle bus," you go where there is help! We moved in with my parents and they helped with my daughter, when I had to go to work (they still do).

If there is a custody agreement involved, it will be hard to accommodate both parties, depending on the situation. Any custody arrangement can be exhausting, infuriating and stressful if the relationship with the other parent is not that great.

However, the key to being successful is to separate your personal relationship with your ex from your co-parenting relationship. This can be hard, especially if you never take time to heal. It was hard
for me in the beginning because I was still trying to figure out
what happened.

Healing is going to take time, but your feelings do not and should not dictate your behavior. When you co-parent, it is not about your feelings or that of your ex-spouse or partner, but rather about your child's happiness, stability and future wellbeing. Keep the kids out of your mess!

If things don't go right or the other parent doesn't do what they are supposed to be doing, don't vent to your child. Children should never know when parents are not agreeing. Seek therapy (there is nothing wrong with that), talk to a friend, workout or write! No matter how old they are, never vent to your child. Definitely don't send messages back and forth through your child, either.

I might have *thought* some bad things in the beginning, but I can honestly say my child has never heard me say anything negative about her dad. She needed to develop her own relationship with
him and for it not to be based off how I felt because we were no longer married.

The next thing to do as a co-parent is to make sure your communication skills are in order. Don't always say the first thing that comes to mind. As the other person is speaking, listen with intent. This can be an ultimate test of maturity! Take turns speaking without interruptions. If you aren't sure about what was said, repeat it for clarification or ask for it to be rephrased. Listening isn't saying that you agree with the other parent, it's allowing him or her to voice their opinion, even if you don't agree with it.

Again, each situation is different, and you have to do what is best for you and your family. Your mindset has to change. Always remember that the focus should always be on the child(ren). You don't always have to meet in person. You can send an email, a text or even a letter through the mail. Just do your best to keep the conversation respectful. No matter how you choose to communicate, think about how your thoughts will come across. You almost have to think of this like a business transaction. In most instances, you will be cordial, respectful and prayerfully neutral. All conversations need to remain about the child(ren). It might be hard in the beginning, but it can be done.

Communicating will also show the child(ren) that you are a united front because they will definitely try you! Even if you have a difficult significant other, communication is a must, but it may seem impossible. You are going to have to learn how to stay in control of your emotions. Again, communication should only be about your child(ren).

Most significant others will know what buttons to push to get you out of character. Practice stress relief techniques to get you through those tough moments. Set boundaries, especially if you didn't go through the court system, as it relates to visits and what you are willing to discuss.

As the child(ren) grows, your initial plan of action is going to change. Even as time progresses, your communication will change and most of the time it is definitely for the better, due to self-growth.

As you grow, the conversation changes from trying to make demands—which we shouldn't do anyway—to asking the other person's opinion. It shows that you value their input as it relates to the child(ren) and that you are keeping the focus on the child(ren).

I used to get so frustrated when my ex would not spend time with our daughter, especially if he was close by. I mean, I clearly didn't have the child by myself. But I had to let it go because I didn't want it to affect me physically or mentally. When he did take the time to hang out with her, I didn't care how long she was gone, I still felt like I had just hit the lottery jackpot!

Co-parent as a team. There is no instructional manual when it comes to raising a child. You pretty much learn as you go, by trial by error. What works for one family may not work for you.

There will be decisions that have to be made concerning your child, and those decisions should include your ex. Newsflash: If you have a court document stating as such, you have to follow it whether you like it or not! When you can do this without arguing, it makes the decision-making process so much easier.

As with communication, the goal with co-parenting is to be consistent! Let me say that again. The goal of co-parenting is to be consistent. Try to keep the rules, discipline ideologies and schedule along the same lines between both households. Will the rules and schedule be exactly the same? Probably not. These are major factors to consider, especially when you don't live in the same state. When rules are generally consistent, it won't be hard for the kids to adjust going from one house to another. You definitely want to try to keep rules related to curfews, TV time and homework issues along the same lines. Remember, you want consistency.

Try to have a similar system for consequences for broken rules. For example, if your child lost TV privileges for a week at one house, the other parent should follow through with the same restriction even though it did not happen at his or her home.

Schedules will differ depending on the situation. For me, my daughter goes to her dad mainly during holidays and the summer.
So, schedule wise, it will be different. Again, do what works best for
your situation.

Co-parenting will also involve making important decisions. For this to work, you both must be open, honest and

straightforward. Who is going to be responsible for medical needs? What about financially taking care of the child(ren)? And what about any concerns relating to education? All of these issues are important! No matter what is decided, keep each other in the loop so there are
no surprises.

- If your child gets in trouble at school, let the other parent know so you both can address the situation, be it together or separately.

- Kids will try to play parents against each other, especially if they think they can get away with it!

- If your child has medicine that is taken on the regular, inform the other parent so the medicine is still being taken while they are in their care.

- Discuss how you will both take care of your child(ren) financially.

- If there is a custody agreement that is court ordered, again, follow that to keep yourself out of trouble.

- Don't withhold funds you are supposed to pay because you and your ex had a disagreement.

- Follow any court rules and regulations that may apply to your situation.

- Compromising will also be key. You will not always see eye to eye, but you can agree to disagree.

So, how do you continue to co-parent when you begin a new relationship? When is the right time to introduce your child to your new partner? Great questions! Naturally, you want everybody to feel comfortable and accepted.

First, remember that your new partner does not replace the biological parent, even if you remarry. When you are dating, don't rush to introduce your child to the person. Kids tend to get attached quick and if you introduce them to every potential suitor, that may pose a problem.

Remember, kids are smarter than what some give them credit for, and they are watching everything you are doing! However, it is ultimately up to you when you feel comfortable introducing your new partner to your child(ren). Ask your child(ren) if they are ready to meet your new partner. Remember, their feelings matter as well.

Boundaries still need to be made not only for the child(ren), but your ex-spouse as well.

*Side note: men and women differ when it comes to introducing their significant other to their kids. Women tend to wait to see where the relationship is going. Men sometimes just go for it and introduce them.*

Ok, back to boundaries with your ex. Is it a requirement that you introduce them to your new partner? No, but it would be considerate. After all, you still have to deal with your ex to some extent and you want everybody to be comfortable.

If this new relationship leads to marriage, then you will need to discuss boundaries and roles the new spouse will have in your child(ren)'s life. Again, the main focus should always be on the child(ren).

Blended families can be tricky. When you remarry, you are a package deal. Not only is your spouse gaining a child(ren), but indirectly, your ex as well. You will have to have open conversations about expectations in order to make both parents feel secure and to possibly prevent any misunderstandings in the future.

This can work and be a beautiful experience for all involved. I am living proof it can work. It hasn't always been pretty, disagreements do happen, but how you handle the situations that arise will show your maturity level.

To the person reading this chapter, you may be in a space where you feel like all hope is lost and there is no way in hell you are going to survive co-parenting. You will. Keep the focus on the child(ren) and keep your feelings out of it! Make sure you heal before, during and after this process.

At one point, when I lived in the same state as my ex, my daughter didn't want to go with him by herself. She wanted me to come along as well. I had to let her know she had to spend time with Daddy, just the two of them. It eventually got easier, and I loved it because I was finally getting time for myself.

Trust me, being a single parent is not for the faint of heart and is definitely not easy! It was a struggle in the beginning, compared to now. The tears, frustrations, prayer, holding my tongue when I wanted to give my ex a piece of my mind...it was hard. But like they say, "You grow through what you go through."

I moved down south when my daughter was three, going on four. It was hard, but I have family here, so it made the transition for me a little easier. My daughter has been flying by herself since the age of five—a whole eight years now!

Preparing her to leave for every other holiday and the entire summer never really gets easy. It definitely wasn't in the beginning; I was both sad and excited to see her go. I know it wasn't easy on her dad either when she had to come back. But we had those hard conversations about the transition back and forth each and
every time.

Did it get easier for him when he remarried? Not at all, but you adapt and, again, keep the focus on your child(ren). For some, it is hard when you become a blended family.

In my situation, we tend to call ourselves a "functional blended family." I talk to my daughter's bonus mom almost as much as I talk to her dad, if not more.

Working as a team definitely has its benefits. Her dad knows about every doctor appointment, he has access to her grades, I mean, he is even listed on the school paperwork. Her teachers know they can reach out to him as well if an issue arises.

We keep the lines of communication open as it relates to our daughter. Her bonus mom would even call and ask if it was ok if she did something with her. I always ask, "What did her dad say?" I mean, I can't control what goes on in their household and vice versa. I even have a painting her bonus mom made over my piano!

When you remove yourself and feelings from the past out of the way, anything is possible.

One of my daughter's sisters is always asking when she is coming down to Alabama. I think it is hilarious. I don't mind, her parents just have to put her on a plane and feel comfortable about doing so.

We share information, and her bonus mom became my go to person! She would remind my daughter to take her medicine because her dad would forget every time she visits. She talks to her and loves on her as if she is her own. She has done her hair for me when I was too sick to make sure it was done before she got there, and she does it when she participates in her summer activities. I can say I am blessed to have the co-parenting relationship that I have with my ex.

I leave you with this: To increase your chance at being successful with co-parenting, let go of the past, focus on your child, communicate, actively listen, support one another, compromise and have a plan in place for holidays and vacations.

Through it all, trust God. I learned that the hard way in the beginning. Putting my trust in God with learning how to co-parent relieved me of the responsibility in trying to make things work out a certain way. That is when discord and frustrations can enter and make co-parenting a difficult task.

Remember, there is a bigger picture! While you may have issues trusting the other parent, the other parent can feel the same as it relates to you. You both love the child(ren) and must remember the goal is to have a healthy family dynamic for them. The goal is to improve daily and remember our child(ren) are watching and so are many others. So let them see Christ in us!

Your journey may not be for you. As a matter of fact, when we go through things, it's not for us, but for somebody else. Today, I pray crazy faith and strength with the aid of His Spirit to do the impossible! Keep your eyes on Him and it will work in favor of all involved, and those breaks are glorious! I miss my daughter during the summer, but just like she looks forward to summer break, I
do too.

Oh, I know this can be scary, but just remember in *1 Peter 5:7* it says, *"Jesus said to cast our cares on Him for he cares about us."* Ask God to show you where fear may reside or in what areas you need to trust in Him more throughout this journey. I promise you He will, and, in the process, He will perfect you, and your child(ren) will thrive in a healthy environment.

*"Do all you can to live in peace with everyone."* *(Romans 12:18.)*

# Listen With Your Heart

## Jazzy Kash

### Femininity in a Male Dominated Industry

Despite how things may seem now, in the early 90's there weren't many women who were filling positions of power. According to Pew Research, there were 0% women CEOs of Fortune 500 Companies, compared to the increase to 7.4% in 2020. Most women were more likely to be hired for clerical or nursing jobs. In 2022, women are finally holding positions of power, and this proves that with time things do show signs of progression. Even more, when we work together as a whole, we can make a difference. Even though the chances seemed slim growing up in the early 90s, I always knew that if I aimed to be a powerful and intelligent woman and committed to pushing the envelope without losing myself, I could prove that women are able to be powerful while still being feminine. To prove this to myself, I participated in extracurricular sports, such as; basketball and cheerleading as well as the

Student Government Association. Athletes were my role models, such as WNBA Player Sheryl Swoops and Olympic Gymnast Dominique Dawes, and as I became a young woman I worked hard to become confident like the powerful women I looked up to.

Our journey into the world as a newborn plays a huge part in our personality and my entrance began with a common illness called Jaundice. What this means is the first week of my life, I didn't look like most babies and I was kept in a NICU for a week until my skin and eyes returned to a normal color. A child normally is accompanied by family and begins learning almost immediately from their parents and caretakers. Without this assistance, a child must rely on their own natural instincts and abilities. Learning from an early age that you are capable of becoming better, awakens an inner understanding that with time everything always works itself out. Based on my delivery into the world, I believe it led me to develop natural traits such as curiosity, strength, courage, and independence at a young age. This also led me to feel a sense of hunger to want more from my life. This realization was due me always feeling a strong connection to God, and through many blessings, God has reminded me that He is always with me. Having this strong faith and self-realization of my value at a very early age was necessary for my upbringing because it awakened my urge to work hard to get more out of my life. This confidence mixed with faith "Godfidence" empowered me to set out in hopes of becoming a role model to future generations of young women, and to pave the way for young girls to believe they too can embrace their "Godfidence" and use this to become a powerful woman.

## Finding Your Femininity

Godfidence will grow as you embrace the transformations and pressures that you will endure on the path to you reaching your highest potential. It's important to network and to make connections in order to grow as a person. Connections help us expand our reach of support as we develop them into some sort of relationship. The basis of building a relationship is to secure a foundation of friendship; most importantly, it has to be based on trust. This helps to form a strong connection no matter the type of relationship, whether it be gaining the trust of others or simply building a foundation of trust in yourself.

Becoming your own best friend, before you can make any true connections will help you to be secure within yourself. In order to gain the trust of others, you must first be willing to accept the truths about yourself, no matter how ugly or painful they may be to face. Embracing all of our past experiences and trusting that all of them have played a role in molding us into the person that we are destined to become.

Along the way, we learn lessons that will help us elevate to new levels and closer to our highest potential. Each day the person that you used to be begins to look less and less like the person you currently are and ultimately you learn to trust yourself. In essence, living in the present moment allows you to go about your day with a sense of knowing. While you are actively exploring the unknown, you can actually begin to relax and trust the journey, because you trust that nothing can stop you from being who you are supposed to become, and you become the person you are supposed to be in its most pure state.

There is beauty in embracing the good and bad, light, and dark, or soft and hard sides to yourself and recognizing the benefits of everything that makes you unique. While there are many other women who may have the same dreams and aspirations, there is no one who is made exactly alike, and what makes you different makes you beautiful.

It can be easy to get caught up in hard lessons, and oftentimes we can hold ourselves back simply by not accepting the situation for what it is. Some lessons aren't as easy to understand in the moment, but in time we begin to acknowledge the barriers in our lives, even if the barrier is yourself! It's important that we forgive our past selves for what we did not know at the time. As we are constantly learning new things every day, each new lesson comes as unfamiliar; it's not until we trust and honor our truth will we seek answers, that we must be prepared for life to test our growth.

When life decides to throw lemons at you, trust your decisions and be compassionate with yourself. The key is to commit to growing at your own pace with a healthy outlet of your choice, whether you decide to exercise, meditate, pray, journal, etc. It's important to be self-aware and reflective in order to apply the lessons that you will carry with you as you mature. It's not until you have self-confidence that will you be able to take your life to new levels of advancements.

Having self-confidence is important, especially because as women in powerful positions this skill alone will help excel in all areas of life. By investing time, effort and even finances, whether that be with education, cosmetic surgeries, a new look or wardrobe into yourself, you are constantly reminding yourself that you are a priority and how you feel about yourself is important.

When you ignore the stagnation that results due to neglecting yourself, you are disrespecting yourself and holding yourself back from greatness. It's your responsibility is to challenge yourself at all stages and to maintain your confidence in order to allow yourself to turn your pain into power.

There will not always be someone there to challenge you to keep going. When you allow yourself to retreat when things get hard, you will then need to be your own best friend and pep yourself up to get back in the game. Remember, where you invest your time and efforts is where you will see improvement, but you cannot improve until you are able to be responsible for yourself. By taking accountability for yourself and consistently showing up, you get to take back control of your life and change the direction. With this uptick in confidence, you will soon notice an increase in your productivity, and you will feel more secure with your decisions. On the flip side, if you fail to honor your truths, you will continue to repeat past mistakes, bad habits, and eventually lower your self-esteem due to neglecting your needs. Confidence is something that has to be practiced constantly and if left untreated over time it can fade. If you continue to believe in yourself through hardships, lessons, and setbacks, your life will drastically elevate to unimaginable heights.

## Taking Ownership of Your *Godfidence*

By now, you should realize that being a woman is no easy feat

and women may wear many crowns in their lifetimes. Especially as a woman in power, you will have to wake up every morning with full confidence in knowing that you are in control of your own destiny, and have the ability to start each day with a powerful approach. A woman of faith knows to speak positively to herself and keep in mind that how she begins and end her day directly impacts the direction of her life. If you wake up to negative thinking, you will most likely have a bad day, unless you actively work to counter that with affirmations of confidence. Even when we don't feel like getting out of bed, we have to decide that we want more for ourselves.

When you reject anything that's negative and harmful to your growth, you will be able to exhibit the highest example of self-love, which is self-mastery because you are able to remind yourself daily that you deserve the best and go after it relentlessly. This constant reminder is your conscience, and it helps you to communicate with your highest self and to honor your true feelings. People will try to get you to fit in, but when you know, you were meant to stand out, you could never allow someone to try to fit you into a box. You are uniquely you and it's up to you to embrace your individuality.

We can place some of the blame of low self-esteem in young women on social media, as it has been the cause of young people caring too much about what others are doing and what people think of them, all while comparing their lives to the lives of others. This has become very detrimental to the growth of young girls, where studies show "The use of the internet, and particularly appearance-focused social media, is associated with heightened body image and eating concerns.

The truth is our society wasn't built to cater to the needs of young girls or to honor strong and powerful women. We live in a man's world because today's society is still being strongly influenced by the likes of masculinity. To this day, there are still more men in power than women, largely due to women feeling the need to conform to societal norms. The truth is, playing small and being average will never be enough to take back our power and use it effectively. With the knowing that feminine energy is the source of creations and together with masculine energy men or women are more than capable to lead, if competent and qualified.

The question that we must ask is why not push the envelope and reach for new heights that were once out of reach for men or women? As many women continue to crush glass ceilings, I am not here to say that it will be easy to accomplish, and of course you will be faced with all types of adversity until we create a new norm. However, with more women embracing their femininity while understanding that their masculinity, will all need to learn how to utilize both aspects in order to work together in harmony.

Aside from people pressuring women to conform to societal norms and traditions, there will also be the pressure to measure up to your male counterparts, it's as if women constantly have to prove that they are firstly competent, let alone qualified. The truth is, leadership skills encompass an array of character traits that assist with overcoming the need to overpower or compete with your male counterparts.

At the beginning of this chapter, we began with the foundation of any relationship is trusting yourself and accepting your truth as well as honoring others' truths and differences. By shifting the focus to forming strong alliances and partnerships and relying on communicating effectively in order to build trust and respect in the workplace, you will succeed in earning the trust of your colleagues, intimate partners, and friendships. By first becoming a great listener you can adjust your understanding to relate to any audience based on respecting alternative opinions and perspectives.

Once you have gained the trust of your peers and not a moment sooner, you can begin to push the envelope and introduce unique ideas while taking into consideration the ideas and thoughts
of others.

In order to rise to leadership as a woman in male dominated industry, your ideas have to be backed with facts, backed in research, and have the ability to be understood and explained. I'll warn you that it's best to be prepared for push back, but if you trust yourself to find solutions as part of a team, have full confidence in your abilities, have taken the time to research the facts and be knowledgeable about the topic, it does not matter if you are a man or woman, people will want to hear what you have to say. People only allow you to lead when they trust that you are prepared to lead. Having a layer of trust will allow you to build strong relationships and it all begins with your relationship with yourself.

Godfidence (n.) - A feeling or consciousness of God's powers or reliance on God's promises; also, the faith or belief that God will act in a right, proper or effective way.

Godfidence is best characterized as being a person who is powerful in actions, strong reliance on God's promises (faith), self-assured, and highly intuitive. By embracing these traits, you will become unstoppable in the eyes of God and anyone who believes in him. Your armor will penetrate the minds and hearts of your enemies when you embrace your God given strengths and know that you are capable of anything that you put your mind to when you trust and believe in the power of creation. There are people who need to see more people who embody the traits of Godfidence because the traits can become contagious if a person admires and respects the person who exhibits the traits. The truth is when you believe in yourself, people want to believe in you too, and it reminds them to believe in themselves.

## Finding Your Tribe

Everyone is walking a journey, yet we all are at different points on our passage to our highest self, therefore no one can tell us that we aren't exactly where we need to be, because we are always learning and growing despite any circumstance beyond our control. We will meet people along our journey who are meant to help us become a better version of ourselves. While we walk this journey of life towards our highest self and ultimate good, we will meet people whose lives we will touch and whose lives will touch us. We carry memories and experiences that will help mold us and open our eyes to the beauty around us. From the moment you find your tribe of supporters that love and support you, life becomes much sweeter.

On the flip side, the wrong people could negatively affect your journey with distractions and take you off track, only if you allow them to. The best way to avoid the wrong people and things is to "stay in your own lane". This means that instead of watching where other people are going, you are staying focused on who is in your vehicle and where you are heading. You won't have to worry about getting off track because the people who belong on your path won't encourage you to change directions, they will motivate you to stay on the path that's best for you. Always keep your eyes towards your future and not back at your past. Your tribe will be the people cheering for you when you make any progress, they will celebrate your accomplishments, and they will triumph with you when
you win.

Anyone who is not helping you, essentially is hurting you. It all boils down to supporters and enemies, and you can notice your enemies by the people who have a lack of care, trust, faith, and confidence; stay away from these people. They will only deprive you of your dreams and rob you of a positive and fulfilled life.

People who walk with Godfidence wear a figurative light on their back, thus we become a beacon for someone walking in your footsteps. It's as though every obstacle you overcome, every solid relationship that you build, the brighter your light appears, and the more people will trust you and you trust yourself. As your light shines, there are people who are inspired by your journey. Someone that came before you will be feeding your light with enlightenment, even if you decide to take the path less travelled. This road will be a little more difficult to navigate because there are not many bright lights guiding the way.

Without guidance from a mentor, therapist, or coach, at times you may struggle with making the right choices. By assuring that you have someone who will assist you on your journey, your goals will become much more obtainable because having a team of confident, competent, and qualified individuals is the keys to success whether they are male or female.

Acknowledging that these traits are best exhibited will require a leader to practice duality in the workplace, let alone life. Honoring a more vulnerable side of yourself in an uncharted territory can feel intimidating at first. Vulnerability can seem scary, because as a woman being more masculine or a man being more feminine can seem irregular but by acknowledging that you don't have all the answers is pivotal to growing as a person. Leaders must be able to relate to their counterparts and audiences, when speaking in public settings.

The best way to be relatable is to be vulnerable. When you hear the word vulnerability, what comes to your mind? Do you consider someone who is vulnerable as being more susceptible to an attack, or harm? Or is vulnerability a way to help you expose yourself to the things that will make you better?

In my opinion, vulnerability is the state of being open and welcoming to advice and enlightenment. Through your pain, you can turn it into power, depending on the way that you portray your vulnerability to others. Are you communicating from a place of openness to new ideas, new people, and new opportunities?

We must grow to a point where these types of lessons that cause us pain are not viewed as a negative. Pain reminds us that everything is temporary, from our feelings to our circumstance, even our personality. By intentionally tending to your pain at the start, you will learn lessons much faster and be able to shine the light of hope on to others coming behind you.

## Empowering Your Audience

How can anyone truly listen if they aren't willing to comprehend?

To be a good leader, you have to be a good listener. It is one thing to hear someone, but to understand and empathize is where many struggle. When you understand yourself, know your audience, and learn how to speak directly to them, it won't matter if you are leading men or women. Dealing with different personalities and people from all walks of life helps you become a well-rounded speaker and leader. Being able to hold conversations will go a long way when networking and making connections. A conversation is an exchange of ideas involving speaking and listening. Most times people will actively listen when they believe there is knowledge or wisdom to gain. Thus, in order to become a great leader in any industry, you must first be able to relate to your audience in order to build trust, all while exhibiting empathy and aiming for understanding of your ideas.

The responsibility rests in the hands of the speaker to deliver a clear message in the most impactful way possible. We have to keep in mind that you do not want to offend, accuse, or belittle your audience in any way. This is where practicing vulnerability will help. It's recommended that you start by sharing a relatable story about yourself or someone you know. By being vulnerable with your audience, you will secure a place of trust in the hearts of your audience and connect on a deeper level. You have to go deep to secure a true bond, and relationships are not built by being on the surface level. Speak with sincerity and honesty and you will find that people will relate to your story and form a connection. Connections defeat the odds and no matter race, sex, or education level, we are human. As long as a speaker is genuine, transparent, and humble, people will listen and process the story.

Being in a position of leadership carries responsibilities because you must understand that your words will impact others. As you lead, you must understand the behaviors of a follower and take into consideration what someone will need to adjust in order to lead effectively. In order to be a great leader, one must be able to follow. Learning from other great leaders is the way true leaders continue to become better at what they do. Great teachers were once amazing students of the craft. A true leader has the ability to build alliances and does so by empowering and motivating others, all while leading by example. Whether you are in a managerial position, a government official, keynote speaker, etc. you will need to always remain humble and levelheaded and aware of feedback and concerns that your team may bring up to be able to find solutions.

## A Feminine Touch

Nothing screams confidence like the ability to articulate your thoughts in a way that is clear, concise, and understandable by your audience. For women, confidence will open doors that would not be available without it, however your ability to communicate effectively will allow you to network with the upper echelons of power. While being timid and mild will only get you so far in your career as a woman, in order to reach a level of power, you will have to be okay with speaking up, standing your ground, and leaving emotions at the door when decision making. If you are able to do this with grace and eloquence, you are already steps ahead. The saying goes, "If you don't stand for something, you will fall for anything." I have reflected often on the meaning of this profound quote and on how important it is to be uneasy to persuade. To earn the respect of your colleagues, it's very important that you stand firmly on your beliefs and values.

The gift of intuition is exclusive to feminine energy and should be utilized in the workplace and any relationship, whether romantic, business, or platonic friendships by both men and women. The gift of strategic planning is exclusive to masculine energy. With both of these energies present in a leader, this is a catalyst for success as a male or female.

Utilizing these skills will allow a person to analyze data and insights about a company to make projections, together with being open to take into consideration the needs, advice, concerns, and criticism of others. Making decisions based on the needs of others will directly tell your team that you care about their needs. No one wants to be led by a "Know-It-All" or someone who thinks their way is the only way to accomplish something, by taking your team into consideration when planning is how you win as a leader.

Teamwork is how leaders succeed! When one wins, everyone wins! So always remember, as leaders we must listen with our heart, not just our minds, take advice and feedback from others, tap into our Godfidence and together we will continue to evolve as a team. Your heart in connection with your mind is where the real connection has to reside.

When you can get them on the same page, you then can take the driver's seat in your life and allow God to navigate you to success, all you must do is follow his directions and light the way for others!

# After All
# Is Said & Done

## Mel V

*"You are not defined by other people's perception of you.
You are defined by how you perceive yourself."*

Deafening silence...as everything moves in slow motion,
effortlessly capturing every hew of pain, rage, sorrow, love,
happiness, misery and confusion.

Sound waves crash against walls of mirrored light,
projecting a spectrum of red... black... Darkness falls as the
unexpected transformation unfolds to a blind eye.

Crashing ocean waves of emotions rush the shore of her
garment that engulfs the beauty hidden beneath the heavy fabric
of despair.

She is drowning...

Slowly being sucked into the current. No, the past.

The tides have beaten the earth's natural polish off the shells that used to conceal the pearl so seamlessly, but now house heavy sand that is quickly compressing the air...

Quicksand.

Stuck...

Fighting a losing battle to grasp bouts of oxygen to fill her lungs, to stay in the place that has destroyed her...

The pressure once used to make diamonds, to build pyramids, to fortify earth, to...

Does no one see the faint reflection of the shadow that once gave shade the size of the Everglades?

Translucent...

Minimalized...

The faint sound of the wings of a hummingbird off in the distance on a windy day.

The tiptoed elephant on broken glass.

The deafening silence of...

The deafening silence of...

Code blue...

Flat Line.

I stare at the three empty Hennessy bottles as I begin to crack open the fourth, and an ashtray full of butts from me trying to smoke away my pain. I ask myself, *How did I get here? How did I get to the point where I feel like I have nothing left to give?*

So hurt that the tears won't even fall; just another feeling of emptiness. A space that I thought I'd never return to.

I look at the bottle of sleeping pills and the bottle of codeine, trying to calculate just how many I could take to end my pain. And somehow even in this moment, even in this feeling of no hope, I still find myself considering how people would look at me or how people may feel about my decision.

How empty it is that I can't even think to end my own life without considering the feelings of other people?

It was like an addiction. The very thing I loved was killing me. My need to look out for or care for others was forcing me to forget about myself. But when did this start? I guess this had always been me. The relentless need to be "Perfect Patty."

Growing up, the expectations were high. It was imbedded into me that average was not me. And being born or groomed to walk in the footsteps of the matriarch was the blueprint for the start of my destruction. It was a bar that left little room for failure. And in true form, I aimed to not disappoint.

The problem with setting yourself up for such high success is that in moments when you don't achieve, the low is *low*.

Even as a child, I was always on the honor roll. A "B" was unacceptable. I didn't get into much trouble, and by most people's standards I was a "perfect child."

And then...enter my stepsister. It's not entirely her fault because me and my mother never had the best relationship, but her existence deemed to challenge the image I strived to set. For the first time in my life, it was like nothing I did was good enough. No matter how hard I tried, there was always room for complaint.

So why even try, right? *Exactly! To hell with this! If Perfect Patty isn't good enough, then let's see how they like the cold-hearted bitch I am about to become.*

From straight As to Ds and Fs, skipping school, drinking, smoking, sex, gangbanging...you name it, I was involved. I was going to be perfect at being bad. Are you getting the pattern here? Even in being the epitome of disrespectful, I was still allowing other people's views of me to define my actions, to define who I'd be.

The funny thing is, my mantra became, "Cold-hearted people live happier lives." But do they really? Was I really happy?

*Abso-freakin-lutely not!* I was miserable. I was dating boys who belittled me at all times, making it clear that I was nothing more than an eight on my best day, or that if I lost weight, I could be so much cuter. I was on a downward spiral, fast.

Reality quickly set in that being defiant wasn't going to get me where I wanted to be, so I decided to try Perfect Patty again. Horrible decision!

I graduated high school and recovered enough from my years of slacking to be able to go to college. In high school I met the one man who accepted me exactly the way I was. For once, I didn't have to be anyone other than my genuine self. It was a feeling that I had never felt before and one that I wouldn't feel again for a long time.

But unfortunately, in the middle of my college matriculation, my world was turned upside down when he was killed in a car accident.

Who was I now? Everyone around me made me feel like I was too young to feel this much hurt, and the guilt of his death haunted me daily as our last conversation was an argument. So, in true fashion, I did what I did best, I put on the mask and went back to being the person everyone else thought I should be.

And although things seemed to look good, those paying close enough attention could see that the weight of it all was transcending into the weight on the scale. Quickly approaching 300 pounds, I faked it, pretending that all was right in my world, and, sadly, the people closest to me believed the façade, or at least pretended they did.

I had mastered "Masked Melonie." She was my consistent representative. She smiled, worked hard, had the upmost confidence and by all accounts had it all together. College graduate with two master's degrees, her own apartment, a car, trips, friends, shopping sprees on her...she was living the life. But who's life?

At 25, I had accomplished more than most, but inside I might as well have been a child. Unsure of who she really was but so consumed with making sure everyone around her was good, that finding herself or living her truth became less and less of a thought and eventually not a thought at all. She had become me. It was no longer a mask; it was who I had become.

I settled on the fact that maybe I wasn't supposed to be happy but that my purpose in life was solely to make others happy, so that's what I did. Whatever people wanted me to be, wanted me to say, needed me to represent, that's what I did.

I closed off my heart to real love and settled for whoever wanted me, even if in their wanting me, it was destroying me. At 25 years old, the newest thing was when was I going to get married and have some kids. So, naturally, I did what was expected.

Funny, most people would have thought that my partner at the time would have made a great husband. We had known each other since childhood and had a great friendship, but as I'd come to learn, great friends don't always make great husbands.

In this case, I was ok with that. I had convinced myself that keeping people at a limited distance would lessen the likelihood of getting hurt. So, I married a man that was "safe." He needed me to "fix" him, so I did what I did best.

It's crazy how it always seems so much easier to help others get their life together, but all the while you can't quite seem to get a handle on your own. It's always hard to look in the mirror when you don't recognize the reflection.

So, there I was, in a relationship with a man who was unemployed, with baby mama drama, in and out of jail, cheating...you name it, he did it. And I stayed. Not only did I stay, but I created a fictious storyline. When he couldn't make family functions because he was in jail, I told family and friends that he was working or with his family. I made sure that he always had the latest fashions so that he could "feel" like a man. I would even give him money before we went out so that he could pay. Here I was, so focused on being Perfect Patty that I was willing to do whatever I needed to do to never give wind of the miserable life I was truly living. I even went on vacations and made it seem like he was
there. Pathetic.

When he cheated on me and had a child, I was pissed. Not because he had a child, but because, *how was I going to explain this?* So, I left.

Good decision, right? Well, it would have been, if I didn't go back. But this time I was determined to make the picture-perfect couple again. So, I married him.

What the hell was I thinking? I had signed myself up for more faking it, more lying and losing more and more of myself by the minute. But to the world, I was a married woman, to a man who "appeared" to love me, so that was good enough to silence critics.

The child he had during our relationship was now living in my home and calling me Mom. I was doing and being what was expected of me. I was a wife and a mother, but the furthest I had ever been from being me.

I had convinced myself that I was happy, but no matter how much I pretended, inside it was killing me...literally. At now 310 pounds, I was in denial. I was in debt from supporting a man and a family that was draining me. I was trying to maintain an image that was costing me more than it was benefiting me, but I kept smiling. I guess I smiled to keep from crying.

I shopped to try and fill all the emptiness I was actually feeling. And I ate...well, I ate because it was the only sense of satisfaction I could muster. And then as if things couldn't get any worse, it did just that and more.

As I approached 30, everyone kept telling me how life changes after 30, but I had no idea just how much mine would actually change. On January 31st of 2013, my soul was literally ripped from my chest. As I sat at my desk at work, my phone rang, and it was as if time immediately stopped.

My father was gone. The man who had been my entire world was no more. Who was I without him? He was my voice of reason, my reality check, my biggest supporter and one of the only people I knew who truly loved me for me, and now he wasn't here. As if I hadn't felt alone before, now I felt utterly invisible.

If the pain of losing him wasn't enough, I then found out that he had taken his own life. He might as well had taken mine too.

*How did I miss this? What could I have done better? Why couldn't I have saved him? Why wasn't I enough for him to stay?* These questions and a thousand others haunted me.

But even in my suffering, I did what I did best. Instead of grieving, I worried about everyone else. *Don't cry too much*

*because your family needs you. Don't tell your grandmother about*
*the suicide because she can't take it.*

When was it going to be ok for me to do what I needed? As
soon as I was old enough, my father had given me direct
instructions on what he wanted when he passed, and I failed him,
even in that moment. I was so concerned with pleasing everyone
else and doing what they wanted me to do that I did everything
he had asked me not to do. And I kept on doing it. And I lost a
little bit more of the little bit of me that I had left.

You're probably thinking, *Damn, you were in your 30s,*
*been through all this and you still hadn't figured out how to put*
*yourself first?*

It's hard to put yourself first when you've lost sight of who
exactly you are.   And sometimes the pain of realizing that, as
much as you think you love yourself, you in fact hate who you are,
so it's just easier to be who and what you've been told you are.
The fear of letting others down, failing or not being enough
suddenly overshadows what you think of yourself.

But don't worry, I eventually started to figure it out. But not
before life punched me in the gut a few more times. After my
father's passing, what I wanted or needed slipped further and
further away. I went into autopilot. I uprooted my life and moved
back to take care of the family home and my grandmother, who at
this point could barely look at me because I reminded her of my
father so much. I took on the responsibility of a house that I
wasn't equipped to handle, but rather than speak up, I did it
anyway and failed miserably.

Just like me, the conditions of the house deteriorated *fast*. It
was almost like the house had become a physical representation
of what was happening to me inside. And then, after losing my
soul, I lost my heart. My grandmother got sick out the blue and
when she did, I felt an immense amount of pressure. Every other

time she had been sick or wouldn't eat, I was the only one that was able to get her to comply, so naturally, my family called me to the hospital to "save" her.

When I arrived, I immediately saw the pain in her eyes. It was as if she wished I hadn't come. I feel like she knew that this time, I wouldn't be able to save her, but just like me she did what she didn't want to do, just to make me feel better. She ate, for the first time in over a day. I thought, *Yes! I did what I was supposed to do. I did what everyone was counting on me to do. I saved grandma.*

But I was wrong. She didn't wake up all day. Once everyone had left and my cousin and I stayed behind, out of nowhere, she woke up and started talking to us as if she had been awake all day. I think she knew I needed that. It was her way of telling me that it wasn't
my fault.

In this conversation, she seemed happy and at peace and all I could think about was if I was to die in that moment, how everyone around me would probably be more concerned with what I'd no longer be able to do for them instead of the fact that I was gone. I wouldn't know what it felt like to be at peace with who I was.

The next day I watched as she passed, and just like that, there was nothing left of me. She had raised me to be strong, determined, valuable, precious and the child of a king. I felt none of those things anymore. I had given up so much of who I was to help others be who they were that I had nothing left.

I had lost the three most important people to me: my father, my grandmother and, most importantly, MYSELF. The people closest to me didn't even notice how bad I was hurting. I had learned to keep everything inside, to smile and pretend.

And then one day, someone that had only known me for a few months walked by me, leaned over and whispered in my ear, "How long are you going to keep wearing that mask? It's time." I was frozen in my stance. *Is it that obvious? Is my secret out? How does*
*he know?*

But a part of me was relieved. Someone had finally seen me. And not the me I had manufactured, but the me that was hurting, that was scared. The me that was dying. And that was the start of my recovery. Yes, recovery. As I mentioned earlier, it was like an addiction. But it was time for me to kick the habit.

First, I had to deal with me. Oftentimes we shy away from seeking help as we think it makes us weak, but the truth is, the strongest thing you can do is love yourself. But just like any other addiction, recovery isn't easy. It was going to take everything I had in me, all the faith I had in God and his unwavering strength and love to get me through.

I started with deciding that 310 pounds was not going to work for me anymore. I was no longer going to hide behind the weight, so my weight loss journey began and I'm glad to say that today, I'm literally half the person I was.

But that wasn't the only weight holding me down, so I filed for divorce. In learning to love myself, I had to recognize what love was supposed to look and feel like, and this was not it. I had conditioned myself to think that leaving my marriage would be considered a failure but winning me back was way more important.

It wasn't an easy decision because I loved the child, I had raised for over four years, and I didn't want to fail her. But what good was I to her in this broken state? I loved her enough to show her that no matter what, she deserved the best and I couldn't do that by continuing to allow myself to be disrespected.

Oh, did I mention that by now he had had another child? Enough was enough. After nine years, it was time to let go and realize that, although far from perfect, I wanted and deserved more than I was getting.

Things were looking up. I was excelling in my career, losing weight, garnering a closer relationship with Christ and rediscovering who I was, but relapses aren't uncommon. When you've been doing something for so long, your mind gets conditioned to think that certain things are normal, even if they are the furthest thing from it. I found myself still settling and calling it happiness. And sometimes the internal battle was too much to bear.

So, one day, after weeks and weeks of limited sleep, stress, overthinking and major heartbreak, I found myself sitting on my bed with a bottle of wine and sleeping pills. Sounds kinda similar to how this chapter began, right? For years, I hadn't been able to understand how my father could have taken his own life. How does someone get that low? But in that moment, I understood more than I wanted to.

I drank and I took a pill and drank and took a pill. I just wanted my mind to turn off.

The next day, I found myself in a state of delirium which ended with me in the hospital, on my father's birthday, nonetheless. By all accounts, I was suicidal.

After I had stabilized, with very limited memory of what had transpired, my doctor came to see me. He told me that it was clear that I had a bigger purpose on earth because with what was in my stomach, I shouldn't have been alive, but there I was. So, I had a choice to make. I could continue on the road I was on and literally think myself to death, or I could choose to take advantage of this second chance I was given and live. And that's what I did.

I decided that day that I was worthy of being here and clearly God thought so too. He saved me for a reason, and now it was up to me to find out why and live in my purpose. I often asked God why he gave me the heart he did, because all it seemed to bring me
was pain.

But now I know that my heart is not the problem; it's the people I chose to share it with. I had to learn that not everyone deserves every part of me. Having a giving and nurturing heart is actually a gift that not everyone possesses. It takes selflessness and strength to be a giver, but it is a gift that needs to be guarded and protected.

A dead battery can't jump a dead battery. I had to learn to get away from people who couldn't charge my spirit when it needed
a jump.

This process wasn't easy. I had to fight against myself and my natural instinct to want to everything for everyone. But it was a fight that had to happen, and it is a fight that I still battle with. But no matter how many rounds, I'll never tap out and I'm determined not to lose.

So how did I push forward? How did I find myself? I wish I could say the answer was simple. And I wish I could tell you that everything in my life is now perfect, but that would be a lie. This is an everyday process for me. And every day I learn something new about how to become the next, better version of myself. So here are my
little gems…

Don't use your energy to worry about what others may think about you, because after all is said and done, what really matters is what *you* think of you. Use your energy to believe, create, trust, grow, manifest, and heal.

Healing...it's hard because you have to dig up everything you've buried. You must take off the mask. You must go to those dark places deep within yourself where you've hidden all the pain, shame, anger, heavy sadness, rejection and loneliness. You must revisit what you're pretending to have overcome.

It is easier said than done because it takes a lot of work. But it's so much better to choose to become healed, healthy and back whole rather than stay broken. Broken pieces cut others.

It takes time, tears, self-reflecting, courage, strength, belief and, most of all, forgiveness. People love to pretend that everything is ok and that nothing bothers them, when in fact their heart is broken, and deep on the inside of their heart, it's screaming and crying for help and peace.

Instead of tapping in and doing the work, most people run to alcohol, drugs, pills, sex or end up making someone else pay. This is not a form of therapy. Go and fix yourself. Heal and love yourself. Learning to love yourself is the most important lesson to learn! Once you do that, the gravity around you shifts.

Boss up! Stop letting people think they can play you. Sit on your throne like you own it. Straighten your crown and let nothing or no one knock it off. Take nothing less than the respect you deserve. It's not the strength of the body that counts, but the strength of the spirit. Strength doesn't come from what you can do. It comes from overcoming the things you once thought you couldn't. It's not easy, but it's necessary.

Being selfless does not mean you care about yourself less! It is ok to put yourself first and make YOU a priority. Saying no is not selfish, it's self-care.

Trust in God's purpose for your life. He doesn't make mistakes. Every trial, every test, every stumble, is a tool...it's a lesson to prepare you for your greatness. He can and will give you everything he promised. You are enough for Him, and He has deemed you worthy.

And after all is said and done, you win!

Made in the USA
Columbia, SC
29 April 2023

15703997R00089